16.50

D1525373

The Gilded Age and Dawn of the Modern

1877–1919

Alamance Community College Library
P.O. Box 8000
Graham, NC 27253

Editorial Advisers

Steven A. Goldberg
Past President, National Council for the Social Studies
Social Studies Department Chair
New Rochelle High School, New Rochelle, New York

Louise A. Hazebrouck
English teacher
Horace Greeley High School, Chappaqua, New York

Deborah Boxer Minchin
Social Studies teacher
New Rochelle High School, New Rochelle, New York

The Gilded Age and Dawn of the Modern

1877–1919

Jeffrey H. Hacker, Editor

M.E.Sharpe
Armonk, New York
London, England

Sharpe
Insights

Copyright © 2014 by M.E. Sharpe, Inc.

All rights reserved. No part of this book may be reproduced in any form
without written permission from the publisher, M.E. Sharpe, Inc.,
80 Business Park Drive, Armonk, New York 10504.

Cover images (clockwise from top left) provided by: Fotosearch/Getty Images; The Granger
Collection, NYC—All rights reserved; Library of Congress

Interior images provided by: The Granger Collection, NYC—All rights reserved, p. 6; The
Granger Collection, NYC—All rights reserved, p. 24; The Granger Collection, NYC—All rights
reserved, p. 40; The Granger Collection, NYC—All rights reserved, p. 52; The Granger Collec-
tion, NYC—All rights reserved, p. 67; The Granger Collection, NYC—All rights reserved, p. 74;
Library of Congress, p. 85; Buyenlarge/Getty Images, p. 109, The Granger Collection, NYC—All
rights reserved, p. 117; AP Photo, p. 126; Library of Congress, p. 139; The Granger Collection,
NYC—All rights reserved, p. 148; Library of Congress, p. 162; Universal History Archive/Getty
Images, p. 181; Fotosearch/Getty Images, p. 188.

The EuroSlavic fonts used to create this work are © 1986–2013 Payne Loving Trust.
EuroSlavic is available from Linguist's Software, Inc.,
www.linguistsoftware.com, P.O. Box 580, Edmonds, WA 98020-0580 USA
tel (425) 775-1130.

Library of Congress Cataloging-in-Publication Data

The Gilded Age and dawn of the modern, 1877–1919 / Jeffrey H. Hacker, editor.
    pages cm. — (History through literature : American voices, American themes) (Sharpe
insights)
    Includes bibliographical references and index.
    ISBN 978-0-7656-8342-7 (cloth : alk. paper) — ISBN 978-0-7656-8326-7 (pbk. : alk. paper)
ISBN 978-0-7656-8327-4 (electronic : alk. paper)
    1. United States—History—1865–1921—Sources. 2. United States—Intellectual life—19th
century—Sources. 3. United States—Intellectual life—20th century—Sources. 4. Literature
and history—United States—History—19th century. 5. Literature and history—United
States—History—20th century. I. Hacker, Jeffrey H., editor of compilation.

E661.G454 2013
973.8—dc23   2013029902

Printed in the United States of America

The paper used in this publication meets the minimum requirements of
American National Standard for Information Sciences
Permanence of Paper for Printed Library Materials,
ANSI Z 39.48-1984.

IBT (c)   10   9   8   7   6   5   4   3   2   1
IBT (p)   10   9   8   7   6   5   4   3   2   1

Contents

Preface

History Through Literature: The Gilded Age and Dawn of the Modern (1877–1919) is the fourth in a six-volume series designed to support interdisciplinary coursework and independent reading in American history and letters. The material presented in each volume is selected and organized to enrich the study of the nation's historical record, its literary heritage, and their mutual influences.

Each volume begins with a chronology that identifies, defines, and places in context the key historical events, literary works, authors' lives, and cultural movements of the period in question. The centerpiece of the volume is a comprehensive overview essay that highlights the era's major historical trends, social and cultural movements, literary voices, and landmark works as reflections of each other and the spirit of the times. The core content comprises 20–30 shorter articles—all drawn from the archives of the Sharpe Reference and Sharpe Online Reference imprints—on lives and works in period literature, including extended excerpts. Special features called *Sidelights* apply a different lens to this exploration, focusing on historical literature as a reflection of both the time of the actual events and the time of the writing. In the present volume, for example, *Sidelights* consider the modernist movement in literature and the arts during the early twentieth century and political interpretations of L. Frank Baum's children's novel *The Wonderful Wizard of Oz* (1900)—a story elevated to cultural icon by the 1939 film version.

Throughout the series, the designation of historical and literary "periods" is not bound by strict start–end dates or specific events (with such notable exceptions as national independence, the Civil War, the Great Depression, and World War II). The lives and works of writers obviously overlap any arbitrarily defined eras, and their styles and themes often evolve in ways that defy neat historical classification. Thus, the designation of historical periods and the selection of subjects in each volume are guided by subjective judgments based on a confluence of factors—historical events, social and economic trends, and the rise and decline of artistic and cultural movements.

This volume, simply enough, begins with the end of Reconstruction in 1877 and concludes with the establishment of peace after World War I in 1919. Clearly, however, the major writers and literary trends of this period are not easily separated from those of the decades preceding or the decades following. Mark Twain, for example, attained national prominence in the late 1860s and early 1870s but produced the main body of his work in the last three-plus decades of his life, to 1910. The American modernist movement was born in the early years of the twentieth century but did not reach fruition until the 1920s.

Thus, taking a thematic rather than a strictly chronological approach, this volume focuses on the emergence of the United States as a modern, urban, industrial, multiethnic power and the literary movements that accompanied that transformation—realism, naturalism, muckraking journalism, local color, and early modernism—as well as the unique perspectives of individual novelists, short-story writers, poets, essayists, and historians.

This was the period in which the United States as we know it today came of age. It was a period of invention—electric power, steam turbines, internal combustion engines, skyscrapers, the lightbulb, the telephone and telegraph, the automobile, powered flight, and motion pictures. It was a period of major industrial innovation and economic growth—with breakthroughs in steel and machine manufacturing producing a seemingly infinite supply of equipment and goods. Manufacturers, in turn, expanded and redesigned their factories for mass production; large corporations raised the necessary capital and limited liability for such ventures. Wealthy industrialists gained monopolies in key industries, such as oil and the railroads, with little oversight of their business practices, working conditions, or treatment of workers. The demand for unskilled and semiskilled labor expanded exponentially, bringing unprecedented numbers of women and children into the industrial workforce. It was also a period of mass urbanization; from 1880 to 1920, the total population of U.S. cities increased from about 28 percent of all residents to just over 51 percent. Immigrants, especially from Europe, accounted for a growing proportion of the urban labor force. This, in turn, gave rise to another defining feature of the period—nativist resistance to aliens.

It has been customary among historians to divide these four formative decades into two periods of about equal duration: the Gilded Age, characterized by ostentatious displays of wealth on the part of wealthy industrialists and by disadvantage, dislocation, and economic distress on the part of the working classes; and the Progressive Era, a period beginning at the turn of the century marked by a whirlwind of social activism and reform. In the view of a growing number of historians, however, the differences between these two periods have been exaggerated. The four decades from the end of Reconstruction to the end of World War I, they suggest, are best understood as a single era of remarkable, multifaceted, socially convulsive change.

The literary voices that animated this period are reproduced in the pages that follow. They are the voices of a runaway boy and a runaway slave rafting on a mighty river; of country girls adrift in the big city; of gold miners and wheat farmers; of Americans in Europe and immigrants on the Great Plains; of privilege and despair; of social reformers and of young African Americans in search of cultural identity and social justice. Settings range from the slums of New York City to the open spaces of the Midwestern prairie; from the meatpacking plants of Chicago to the railroads of California; from Creole Louisiana to Old New York; from small-town New England to small-town Ohio. Recurring themes include rags-to-riches morality and who qualifies for the American Dream; corporate greed, personal vice, and who will be punished; and the widening chasm between social classes as the frontier closed and a diversifying population moved into factories, cities, and the modern technological age.

Inevitably, great works of literature stand as vital documents of political, social, cultural, and intellectual history no less than as products of individual creative inspiration. The authors and works showcased in this volume—representing prose fiction, poetry, social commentary, and history—are offered as compelling narratives in the study of history through literature and the appreciation of literature through history.

Chronology

1873 *The Gilded Age: A Tale of Today,* written collaboratively by Mark Twain and Charles Dudley Warner, satirizes greed, ostentation, and corruption in government and business during the post–Civil War period. The term "Gilded Age" will be used to designate the era in U.S. history—and its defining social trends—to the turn of the twentieth century.

1877 The Compromise of 1877 ends Reconstruction in the South; Republican president Rutherford B. Hayes removes the last federal troops from Louisiana and South Carolina.

In the final year of an economic depression that began with the Panic of 1873, federal and state militias suppress a national railroad strike that paralyzed transportation for 45 days.

Expatriate author and critic Henry James publishes *The American,* the first of his novels about an innocent American confronting European society and culture.

1881 Republican president James A. Garfield dies of an assassin's bullet on September 19, just 200 days after taking office; Chester A. Arthur accedes to the presidency.

Henry James publishes what many will consider his masterpiece novel, *The Portrait of a Lady.*

1882 Congress passes and President Chester A. Arthur signs the Chinese Exclusion Act, barring the immigration of Chinese workers for 10 years.

1884   Grover Cleveland defeats Republican James G. Blaine to become the first Democratic president since before the Civil War.

Mark Twain publishes *Adventures of Huckleberry Finn.*

1885   The first skyscraper with an entirely steel frame, the 10-story Home Insurance Company Building, opens in Chicago.

William Dean Howells, "the father of American literary realism," publishes *The Rise of Silas Lapham,* a novel critical of Gilded Age materialism and superficiality.

1886   A bomb explodes in Chicago's Haymarket Square as police try to disperse a May rally in support of the eight-hour workday; immigrant German "anarchists" are charged with the bombing on tenuous evidence. Also in May, American Federation of Labor is founded in Columbus, Ohio. In October, the Statue of Liberty is dedicated in New York.

1887   Richmond, Virginia, becomes the first U.S. city to install an electric trolley system.

Edward Bellamy publishes his utopian science-fiction novel *Looking Backward: 2000–1887,* which sparks popular interest in socialism.

1890   According to the U.S. Census Bureau, the spread of the population across the country has caused the disappearance of the American frontier.

Mississippi becomes the first state to disenfranchise African Americans. Wyoming becomes the first state to grant women the right to vote. U.S. cavalrymen open fire on Lakota Indians in the Wounded Knee Massacre, the last major battle in the Indian Wars.

Jacob Riis's *How the Other Half Lives* exposes tenement life in New York City.

1892   The immigration processing station opens on Ellis Island in New York Harbor; in the next 60 years, more than 12 million immigrants will be processed on Ellis Island.

Charlotte Perkins Gilman publishes "The Yellow Wallpaper," a chilling short story about a woman's descent into madness.

1893   A collapse of the railroad industry triggers a stock market panic and the worst economic depression in the nation's history to date. In June, Eugene V. Debs establishes the American Railway Union, the largest industrial labor organization of the time.

The Columbian Exposition, a celebration of America's technological and industrial progress and the four-hundredth anniversary of Columbus's arrival, is held in Chicago. At the exposition, Frederick Jackson Turner presents his landmark paper "The Significance of the Frontier in American History."

Stephen Crane publishes *Maggie: A Girl of the Streets*, a brutally naturalistic novel of life in the slums of New York City. Kate Chopin's "Désirée's Baby," a story of miscegenation in antebellum Creole Louisiana, appears in *Vogue* magazine. And in an article titled "The Gospel of Wealth," industrialist Andrew Carnegie argues that wealth is available to anyone who is willing to work for it but that it carries a responsibility to society.

1895   Stephen Crane publishes his Civil War novel *The Red Badge of Courage,* which earns critical acclaim for its realistic account of battle through the eyes of a Union private.

1896   Republican William McKinley defeats pro-silver populist William Jennings Bryan for the U.S. presidency; he will do so again in 1900.

In the case of *Plessy v. Ferguson,* the U.S. Supreme Court upholds a Louisiana segregation law under the doctrine of "separate but equal."

The Klondike Gold Rush begins in northwestern Canada and Alaska.

1898   The Spanish-American War signals the emergence of the United States as a world power, resulting in a dramatic expansion of the nation's overseas possessions and a more global, imperialistic vision of its role in the world.

1899   Kate Chopin publishes her proto-feminist novel *The Awakening*. Philosopher John Dewey calls for educational reform in *The School and Society*. Sociologist Thorstein Veblen assails "conspicuous consumption" in *The Theory of the Leisure Class.*

1900   Theodore Dreiser shocks readers with his first novel, *Sister Carrie,* about a country girl who goes to the big city and loses her virtue.

L. Frank Baum publishes a highly successful children's novel titled *The Wonderful Wizard of Oz;* Baum will go on to write a musical stage version and 13 book sequels.

1901   President William McKinley is assassinated by an anarchist at the Pan-American Exposition in Buffalo, New York, in September; Theodore Roosevelt becomes president.

U.S. Steel Corporation is founded. The Socialist Party of America is formed.

Frank Norris publishes *The Octopus,* a grim naturalistic novel about the conflict between wheat growers and the railroad in California. Booker T. Washington, founder of the Tuskegee Institute (1881) and proponent of the gradualist approach to racial integration, publishes his autobiography, *Up from Slavery.*

1903   Orville and Wilbur Wright make the first successful engine-powered airplane flight at Kitty Hawk, North Carolina.

Jack London publishes *The Call of the Wild,* a stunning adventure novel about the struggle for survival of a sled dog named

Buck in the Klondike Gold Rush. African American scholar and civil rights advocate W.E.B. Du Bois issues *The Souls of Black Folk,* a collection of essays about the black experience and the path to racial equality.

1904   Two classics of muckraking journalism that began as magazine series are published in book form: Ida Tarbell's *The History of the Standard Oil Company,* an exposé of John D. Rockefeller's petroleum monopoly, and Lincoln Steffens's *The Shame of the Cities,* documenting urban political corruption.

1906   Upton Sinclair's muckraking novel *The Jungle,* which exposes the unsanitary conditions and exploitation of workers in the Chicago meatpacking industry, causes a public outcry. Amid the clamor, President Theodore Roosevelt coins the term "muckraker" in a spring speech and signs the Pure Food and Drug Act and Meat Inspection Act into law in June.

The San Francisco earthquake and ensuing fires leave more than 3,000 people dead and the city in ruins.

1908   The Ford Motor Company begins producing the Model T. The General Motors Company is founded.

1910   Black Americans are disenfranchised in all Southern states. The newly formed National Association for the Advancement of Colored People launches its official monthly magazine, *The Crisis,* with W.E.B. Du Bois as editor in chief.

Social reformer Jane Addams publishes *Twenty Years at Hull-House,* an account of her pioneering work at a Chicago settlement house and her theories of social welfare.

1911   The U.S. Supreme Court dissolves the Standard Oil Company under the Sherman Anti-Trust Act (1890) and divides it into competing regional firms.

The Triangle Shirtwaist Factory fire in New York City takes the lives of 146 sweatshop workers, most of them young immigrant women; the incident leads to state laws requiring improved safety standards and working conditions.

Edith Wharton publishes her popular short novel *Ethan Frome,* a bleak story of thwarted love and stifling convention in a small Massachusetts town. Ambrose Bierce publishes *The Devil's Dictionary.*

1912   Dissident Republicans led by Theodore Roosevelt bolt the party convention and form the Progressive, or Bull Moose, Party. Membership in the Socialist Party of America reaches 118,000. Democrat Woodrow Wilson is elected president in an unusual four-way contest.

The "unsinkable" British ocean liner *Titanic* goes down in the North Atlantic after striking an iceberg; some 1,500 passengers and crew members are lost.

Theodore Dreiser, the preeminent exponent of American literary naturalism, publishes *The Financier,* the first novel in his Cowperwood Trilogy (or Trilogy of Desire); it will be followed by *The Titan* (1914) and *The Stoic* (1947).

1913   The Armory Show, an art exhibition held in New York, Chicago, and Boston, introduces American audiences to the modernist movement popular in Europe.

1914   World War I erupts in Europe. The Panama Canal is formally opened to traffic.

1915   A German U-boat sinks the HMS *Lusitania* off the Irish coast; among the 1,200 killed are 128 Americans, testing the U.S. policy of nonintervention in Europe.

The first transcontinental telephone call is completed between Alexander Graham Bell in New York and Thomas Watson in San Francisco.

D.W. Griffith debuts his controversial silent film about the Ku Klux Klan, *The Birth of a Nation,* based on Thomas Dixon's novel *The Clansman* (1905). Edgar Lee Masters writes *Spoon River Anthology,* a collection of free-verse poems about the lives of 212 people buried in a small Midwestern town. T.S. Eliot enters the literary scene with his early modernist poem "The Love Song of J. Alfred Prufrock."

1916   Jeannette Rankin of Montana becomes the first woman elected to the U.S. House of Representatives. The National Woman's Party is founded.

1917   The United States declares war on Germany on April 6 and establishes the Selective Service to conscript troops for the fighting in Europe.

The Espionage Act is passed to prohibit the obstruction of military operations or recruitment. Anarchist Emma Goldman is jailed for two years for obstructing the draft.

1918   World War I comes to an end with the armistice of November 11.

A deadly flu pandemic spreads around the world. By the middle of the following year, the disease has killed up to 50 million people globally and 675,000 in the United States.

The Education of Henry Adams, an iconic work of autobiography and intellectual history, is published after the author's death on March 27. Willa Cather's *My Ántonia* completes her Prairie Trilogy, following *O Pioneers!* (1913) and *The Song of the Lark* (1915).

1919   Victorious Allies meet in Paris to set the terms of peace after World War I. The Treaty of Versailles, including a covenant to establish the League of Nations, is signed on June 28. The U.S. Congress later votes against ratification.

The Eighteenth Amendment, prohibiting the "manufacture, sale, or transportation" of alcoholic beverages, is ratified. Congress also passes the Nineteenth Amendment, granting women the right to vote. Both take effect the following year.

Sherwood Anderson publishes *Winesburg, Ohio,* a series of connected short stories about residents of a small town in Ohio; in theme and technique, it is a groundbreaking work of American modernist fiction.

The Gilded Age and Dawn of the Modern

1877–1919

Literature of the Gilded Age and Progressive Era

The four decades between the end of Reconstruction in 1877 and the end of World War I in 1919 were a period of breathtaking growth and change for the United States. The national population more than doubled, from less than 50 million to over 100 million, as 10 new Western states joined the Union and tens of millions of hopeful immigrants set foot on U.S. shores. The foundation of the American economy and way of life shifted from farming, the skilled trades, and small manufacturing to large-scale industry and mass production. With that came an exodus to Northern cities that would continue until the mid-twentieth century. By 1920, according to the U.S. census, more Americans were living in "urban" places than in "rural" ones for the first time.

During this period of sweeping social transformation, big business and big government became the dominant national institutions. Virtually every aspect of American life—production, consumption, transportation, communication, and recreation—became "mass." At a bewildering rate for some, technology brought new marvels to industry and home life that both fueled the economic expansion and increased leisure time. Looking back on his 60 years in 1920, novelist Hamlin Garland proclaimed, "I have seen more of change in certain directions than all the men from Julius Caesar to Abraham Lincoln." During his lifetime, Garland wrote, he had witnessed "the reaping hook develop into the combined reaper and thresher, the ox-team give way to the automobile, the telegraph to the radio, and the balloon to the flying machine."

In short, it was during this period that the nation as we know it today came of age. By the signing of the Treaty of Versailles ending World War I in June 1919, the United States had emerged as a modern, urban, industrial, multiethnic power that stretched from coast to coast and claimed extensive foreign possessions.

The literature produced in America during this period is similarly notable for its energy, variety, innovation, and sheer proliferation. In countless ways, the writing of the era reflects the social, cultural, economic, and technological changes that transformed the country. As minorities and immigrants flooded into cities and packed into tenement squalor, antebellum romanticism gave way to a gritty realism and strident naturalism in fiction and a hard-hitting investigative zeal on the part of muckraking journalists. As the census of 1890 reported the disappearance of the Western frontier, writers of the "local-color" movement captured the geography and flavor of remote regions, from the bayous of Louisiana to the Klondike of Alaska. With the dislocations of industrial life and the Great War came early works of modernism in the 1910s. Throughout, minority, immigrant, and woman writers brought new voices and literary perspectives.

> *"I have seen more of change in certain directions than all the men from Julius Caesar to Abraham Lincoln."*
> **—Hamlin Garland**

The combination of social change and technological advancement also ushered in new forms of writing and new vehicles of dissemination. With the advent of free, mandatory public education—a hallmark of Progressive Era reform—came a sharp rise in national literacy and an expanding audience for literature. Coinciding with this were advances in printing technology, declines in paper prices, and a burgeoning railroad network that triggered an explosion of newspapers, illustrated national magazines, and mass-produced books. The ascendant middle class took a particular liking to sentimental romances (often in serial newspaper installments), historical novels (many focusing on the Revolutionary War), and dime novels (cheap paperbacks initially featuring cowboys and frontiersmen and, later, detectives). For more "high-brow" readers, the Little Magazine movement provided new vehicles for nonconformist literature, cultural criticism, and social commentary.

Realism, Regionalism, and Naturalism

Many of the great literary achievements of the Gilded Age and Progressive Era were made in fiction, specifically in novellas and novels offering realistic portrayals of life in diverse postwar settings.

The rapid expansion of population, territory, and industrial power brought equally rapid change to rural and urban landscapes, the living and working conditions of the laboring class, and the plight of groups with the least resources to stand up to power, corruption, and greed. Works of literary realism thus marked a break from the sentimental romanticism of the pre–Civil War era and aspired to represent the true motives and impulses of real men and women in real situations and settings. These were as diverse as the Mississippi River towns of Tom Sawyer and Huckleberry Finn, whose creator was the first American writer to emerge from the Western frontier; the bayous of Cajun/Creole country in Natchitoches Parish, Louisiana, as conjured by Kate Chopin; and the Victorian parlors of London and Paris where naïve, unsophisticated Americans confront Old World aristocracy in the novels of Henry James. In every instance, vernacular plays a central role in establishing the authenticity of character and location.

The staunchest advocate of American realism, as well as one of its most accomplished practitioners, was the literary critic and novelist William Dean Howells. His 1885 novel *The Rise of Silas Lapham*, a rags-to-riches story that indicts Gilded Age business practices as it upends frivolous sentimentality, aspires to the principle of realism as articulated in his 1891 essay collection *Criticism and Fiction*. A novel, Howells maintained, should be "nothing more and nothing less than the truthful treatment of material." Eager to free American fiction from stifling romantic conventions, he called on writers to minimize sensational incidents and dire catastrophes; concentrate on the average moments of everyday life; emphasize character rather than an action-filled plot; avoid authorial intrusions; and express the values of common men and women rather than those of mythic or legendary beings.

Influenced by foreign writers such as Honoré de Balzac in France and Ivan Turgenev in Russia, American realism found uniquely diverse expression in the local-color movement, or literary regionalism. Local-color writing, typically in short-story form, focuses on the physical landscape, native culture, way of life, manners, and dialect of a particular region. While setting is a central element in all works of fiction, local-color writing is conceived largely or primarily to give readers a faithful description of the people, natural features, and everyday life in a faraway place.

With the national domain extending from the Atlantic to the Pacific—but the frontier now closing—writers of fiction depicted the great regional and cultural diversity of American life before industry, commerce, and communication on a mass scale began to conjoin locations and homogenize ways of life. Prominent regional writers of the late nineteenth century evoked the Far West (Bret Harte, Mark Twain, and Owen Wister); the Midwest (Willa Cather, Edward Eggleston, and Hamlin Garland); the South (Kate Chopin, George Washington Cable, Joel Chandler Harris, and Mary Noailles Murfree); and even New England and New York (Mary E. Wilkins Freeman, Harriet Beecher Stowe, Sarah Orne Jewett, and Edith Wharton). Especially noteworthy among local-color stories are Harte's "The Luck of Roaring Camp" (1868), Jewett's "A White Heron" (1886), Harris's "Free Joe and the Rest of the World" (1887), and Chopin's "Desirée's Baby" (1893).

By the decade of the 1890s, the vigor and power of literary realism had begun to wane in the eyes of some writers and literary critics. In an essay titled "A Plea for Romantic Fiction," muckraking novelist Frank Norris sarcastically declared, "Realism is minute; it is the drama of a broken teacup, the tragedy of a walk down the block, the excitement of an afternoon call, the adventure of an invitation to dinner." Others complained specifically of Howells's brand of realism and its preoccupation with the "smiling aspects" of American life. With so many members of society living and working in the direst conditions while wealthy industrialists and machine politicians enjoyed unfettered wealth and power, disaffected writers of fiction turned to a grittier, more intense brand of realism with an underlying pessimism about human nature but a strong social conscience—a new literary movement called naturalism.

Literary naturalism, which succeeded realism as the dominant trend in American fiction around the turn of the twentieth century, shares its emphasis on unvarnished, unsentimental truth in the everyday lives of ordinary people. Beyond that, however, it brings a deterministic view to human behavior in the spirit of Charles Darwin's *Origin of Species* (1859), Herbert Spencer's concept of Social Darwinism, and Émile Zola's *The Experimental Novel* (1880). The naturalists believed that human beings are fundamentally controlled by heredity, unconscious desires, or social and economic environment. Naturalist novels focus specifically on the plight of the lower classes, the dispossessed, and the marginalized at the hands of the rich, the powerful, and a dehumanizing world over which they have no control.

Foremost among American naturalists were Stephen Crane, Theodore Dreiser, Jack London, and Frank Norris. Any list of their principal contributions to naturalistic fiction would have to include Crane's *Maggie: A Girl of the Streets* (1893) and *The Red Badge of Courage* (1895); Dreiser's *Sister Carrie* (1900), *The Financier* (1912), and *An American Tragedy* (1925); London's *The Call of the Wild* (1903) and *The Sea-Wolf* (1904); and Norris's *The Octopus* (1901) and *The Pit* (1903). Novels such as these not only enriched the era in which they were published but also laid the groundwork for the candid, gritty, sometimes disturbing literature of modernist authors such as Ernest Hemingway, John Dos Passos, John Steinbeck, and Richard Wright.

Popular Fiction and the American Dream

In the new realm of popular fiction, the best-known author from the 1870s to 1890s was Horatio Alger, Jr., whose *Ragged Dick; or, Street Life in New York* (1868) began a run of more than 135 novels for boys that perpetuated the great American tropes of the "self-made man," "rugged individualism," and the Protestant work ethic. The heroes of his stories, typically upstanding young men, inevitably achieve material success and middle-class respectability by means of hard work, perseverance, and luck. These repeated outcomes stand in contrast to the "success" of Howells's title character Silas Lapham, who earns a fortune in the paint business but cannot break into Boston's upper-class society because of his poor background and lack of social graces.

At the far end of the socioeconomic spectrum, belying *any* semblance of the American Dream or social justice, are two title characters in landmark works of naturalistic fiction. Both are young females: Crane's Maggie, an Irish working girl in the Bowery section of New York City who is drawn into a life of prostitution; and Dreiser's "Sister" Carrie Meeber, a naïve country girl who moves to Chicago, parlays illicit relationships with two men into success as an actress, but suffers to the end with an unnamed, unsatis-

A son of the American frontier and small-town life, Mark Twain both captured and shaped the national character with his down-to-earth egalitarian spirit, irreverent humor, and ear for dialect.

fied desire. Others for whom the American Dream proves empty include the title character in Edwin Arlington Robinson's poem "Richard Cory"; the grotesques in Sherwood Anderson's short-story sequence *Winesburg, Ohio* (1919); and the African Americans in Paul Laurence Dunbar's lyric verse and W.E.B. Du Bois's *The Souls of Black Folk* (1903).

Preeminent among period authors whose works earned both mass commercial appeal and critical acclaim were Mark Twain and

Jack London, both of whom achieved international celebrity. In the latter case, success came first with the publication of broad-appeal adventure stories in mass-circulation magazines. Meanwhile, favorite books of the Gilded Age had included Louisa May Alcott's *Little Women* (1868–1869), Lew Wallace's *Ben Hur* (1880), Helen Hunt Jackson's *Ramona* (1884), Frances Hodgson Burnett's *Little Lord Fauntleroy* (1886), Anthony Hope's *Prisoner of Zenda* (1894), and Charles Major's *When Knighthood Was in Flower* (1898). By the end of the century, the most successful works had been dubbed "best-sellers."

After 1900, fiction that previously had been published in dime novels began to appear in so-called pulp magazines. In addition, a new generation of popular novelists came on the scene, producing book series of enduring appeal: L. Frank Baum, author of *The Wonderful Wizard of Oz* (1900) and 13 sequels; mystery writer Mary Roberts Rinehart ("the American Agatha Christie"); Western writer Zane Grey; and Edgar Rice Burroughs, creator of multiple adventure series and the jungle hero Tarzan.

Voices Lifting: Minorities, Immigrants, Women

Among minority groups, African Americans made perhaps the most substantial contributions to American letters, while continuing to expand the breadth, popular appeal, and sheer quantity of their published works. *Sketches of Southern Life* (1872) by Frances Ellen Watkins Harper was a literary landmark of the Reconstruction era, evoking the experience of freed slaves in the South in lyric poetry. Harper's *Iola Leroy* (1892) and Pauline Hopkins's *Contending Forces* (1900) were among the earliest novels written by black women. Charles W. Chesnutt's story collection *The Conjure Woman* (1899) demonstrated a superb talent in the art of short fiction.

Alternating between black vernacular in the realist-naturalist mode and the conventional language of the white genteel tradition, Paul Laurence Dunbar emerged as the principal African American poet of the late nineteenth century and the first black author to gain a national crossover audience. But by far the two most noteworthy books by African Americans at the turn of the century were works of nonfiction that captured a central debate within the black community.

Booker T. Washington's autobiographical *Up from Slavery* (1901) recounts the obstacles he overcame to earn an education and establish a vocational training school for young African Americans; self-help and hard work, rather than agitation and confrontation, he maintained, is the best path to black advancement. Repudiating that conciliatory approach, W.E.B. Du Bois's *The Souls of Black Folk* (1903), a collection of essays, sketches, and "sorrow songs," emphasizes the importance of racial pride and intellectual development among African American youth, arguing that the path to liberation lies in the leadership of an educated black elite.

With Asian immigration skyrocketing in the middle and latter decades of the nineteenth century, several new ethnic voices gained prominence: Japanese-born Sadakichi Hartmann, a flamboyant poet, playwright, and disciple of Walt Whitman; Edith Eaton, a short-story writer and journalist who adopted the Cantonese pen name Sui Sin Far for her pieces on the Chinese American experience; and her sister, Winnifred Eaton, a novelist who wrote under a Japanese-sounding pseudonym, Onoto Watanna. Notable among Native American authors of the period were Zitkala-Sa (missionary name Gertrude Simmons Bonnin), who recorded the legends of her Sioux people; Santee Dakota historian Charles A. Eastman; Cherokee fiction writer and magazine editor John Oskison; and Paiute activist and author Sarah Winnemucca. On the whole, these individuals rejected the federal policy of assimilating Indians into mainstream white society and sought ways to preserve tribal customs and traditions through their writing.

With the American women's movement rising from infancy in the antebellum era to the achievement of voting rights with the Nineteenth Amendment to the U.S. Constitution in 1920, the female perspective in literature likewise gained steadily in prominence and influence. That advancement culminated in the work of at least three masters of literary fiction around or after the turn of the twentieth century whose novels have entered the American canon: Kate Chopin's scandalous narrative of female sexual desire and adultery in *The Awakening* (1899); Willa Cather's nostalgic re-creations of pioneer life, regional landscape, and European immigrant culture on the Great Plains in her Prairie Trilogy: *O Pioneers!* (1913), *The Song of the Lark* (1915), and *My Ántonia* (1918); and Edith Wharton's urbane novels of Old New York high society, including *House of Mirth* (1905) and *The Age of Innocence* (1920).

Nonfiction

Much as popular magazines provided a new outlet for writers of literary and popular fiction, so they created a vehicle for critically minded investigative journalists to expose the ills of modern society. These "muckrakers," as President Theodore Roosevelt dubbed them, published their reports of corporate greed and government corruption in magazine and newspaper serials, sometimes followed by book versions. Such was the case with Jacob Riis's *How the Other Half Lives* (1890), which excoriated the dreadful conditions in New York City tenements; Ida Tarbell's *The History of the Standard Oil Company* (1904); and Lincoln Steffens's *The Shame of the Cities* (1904)—all classics of the genre. Upton Sinclair's naturalistic novel *The Jungle* (1906), decrying the grim working conditions and public health threat of Chicago's meatpacking industry, is considered the quintessential work of muckraking fiction.

The reformist spirit of the Progressive Era also found expression in an abundance of scholarly works with lasting impact, among them Thorstein Veblen's *The Theory of the Leisure Class* (1899), a biting criticism of materialism, the concentration of wealth, and "conspicuous consumption" in an uncontrolled capitalist system; Charlotte Perkins Gilman's *Women and Economics* (1898), a groundbreaking study of the role of women in society subtitled "A Study of the Economic Relation Between Men and Women as a Factor in Social Evolution"; and John Dewey's *Democracy and Education* (1916), one of his several books that recognized public schooling as a vital agency of democratic society. Perhaps the most respected American intellectual of his time, Dewey joined logician Charles Sanders Peirce and psychologist and philosopher William James as leading proponents of the distinctly American philosophical movement known as pragmatism, ascendant from the 1870s into the 1920s.

Not to be overlooked among the nonfiction achievements of this era are three notable autobiographies: *The Life and Times of Frederick Douglass* (1881), the author's third and final account of his slave experiences; Ulysses S. Grant's *Personal Memoirs* (2 vols., 1885–1886), a narrative highly praised by critic Edmund Wilson; and *The Education of Henry Adams* (1918), one of the most celebrated personal records and meditations on history in American literature.

Poetry

The two foremost American poets of the nineteenth century—Walt Whitman and Emily Dickinson—both began writing in the antebellum era, reached lyrical maturity during the Civil War years, and remained productive into the 1870s. Assuming the mantle into the early twentieth century were New Englander Edwin Arlington Robinson (known especially for his "Tilbury Town cycle"); Vachel Lindsay, the "singing poet" and performance artist; Edgar Lee Masters (*Spoon River Anthology,* 1915); the aforementioned Paul Laurence Dunbar; Sara Teasdale; and, early in long, productive careers, Robert Frost, William Carlos Williams, Hilda Doolittle (H.D.), and Carl Sandburg.

Heralding a vibrant new era, Harriet Monroe's *Poetry: A Magazine of Verse,* founded in Chicago in 1912, provided a vehicle for these and other up-and-coming poets. In June 1915, it published the seminal work of twentieth-century modernist verse, T.S. Eliot's "The Love Song of J. Alfred Prufrock."

Donald D. Kummings and Jeff Hacker

See also: Muckraking; Naturalism; Realism

◇◇◇

Sidelight

Modern and Modernism—Terms of Art

The term "modern" as employed by historians has long confounded readers with the assortment of time frames it has been used to denote: the post–World War II era, the decades since the turn of the twentieth century, the period after the Industrial Revolution, and all of Western history since the end of the Middle Ages (whenever that was). For students of American history and culture, the term "modernism"—representing a specific movement in literature and the arts—only adds to the confusion.

By whatever process scholars designate periods of history, the final decades of the nineteenth century clearly brought sweeping changes to the United States. Looking back, the transformation of America from a growing but isolated republic, healing from civil war, into a unified transcontinental nation, burgeoning industrial power, engine of technological innovation, and imperial global presence marked the beginning of an era that bears the essential features of what we recognize as *modern America.*

The rapid modernization of American life—territorial expansion, population growth, economic and technological development, urbanization, and ethnic diversification—also brought unprecedented social upheaval. Corporate power and wealth accrued in the hands of industrialists who held monopolies in oil, steel, the railroads, and banking and finance; some called them "robber barons." As chronicled by muckraking journalists and novelists in the naturalistic style, the urban working class— whose ranks swelled with women and children, many of them immigrants—labored long hours under unsafe conditions and lived in tenement squalor. On the prairie, homesteaders and small farmers had little defense against the crippling freight prices imposed by railroad giants. Government corruption at every level ratified the inequities.

At the turn of the twentieth century, around the time that President Theodore Roosevelt began taking on corporate monopolies and ushering in an era of progressive reform, writers and artists of all kinds began experimenting with new forms of expression that rejected what they regarded as materialistic, conformist nineteenth-century values and that overthrew conventional representations of reality. In embracing the modern, a new generation of writers, poets, painters, sculptors, composers, dancers, and designers pursued more radical styles, unfettered by artistic rules and standards, that overturned traditional definitions of art. This movement, in all its varied and protean forms, would come to be called *modernism.*

Influenced by such revolutionary thinkers as Karl Marx, Sigmund Freud, and Friedrich Nietzsche, European artists and writers in the early twentieth century experimented with such new styles of creative expression as Cubist painting and sculpture (Pablo Picasso, Georges Braque, Marcel Duchamp); Fauvist and Expressionist painting (Henri Matisse and Wassily Kandinsky); stream-of-consciousness writing (James Joyce and Marcel Proust); atonal music (Arnold Schoenberg); and Igor Stravinsky's avant-garde ballet score *The Rite of Spring*.

A turning point in America came in February 1913 with the International Exhibition of Modern Art, or Armory Show, in New York City. The exhibition introduced U.S. audiences, accustomed to easy-to-understand realistic paintings, to the works of European modernists. Many visitors were shocked, still more of them befuddled. Among American artists of all kinds, the creative freedom and energy represented by the Armory Show opened new realms of possibility.

Modernism in America found expression in a variety of formats and media. In painting, Georgia O'Keeffe, Charles Demuth, and Marsden Hartley, among others, broke new ground in abstraction. O'Keeffe's husband, Alfred Stieglitz, pioneered photography as an art form and championed the modernist creations of sculptors and painters as well as photographers. Loie Fuller and Isadora Duncan explored free dance. The innovative architectural designs of Frank Lloyd Wright directly influenced modernist schools that later emerged in Europe.

Literary modernism took hold in the United States in the second decade of the twentieth century and came to full fruition in the 1920s. Trendsetting early works included T.S. Eliot's "The Love Song of J. Alfred Prufrock" (1915), a poem in the form of interior monologue; the imagist verse of Hilda Doolittle (H.D.) and Ezra Pound; the experimental prose of expatriate salon host and arts patron Gertrude Stein; and Sherwood Anderson's *Winesburg, Ohio* (1919), a connected series of short stories directly influenced by psychoanalytic theory. Bolstering the movement was the rise of literary magazines and other outlets for cultural criticism, avant-garde theory, and political commentary, including *The Masses* (founded 1911), *Poetry* (1912), *The New Republic* (1914), and *The Seven Arts* (1916).

By all accounts, the term "modernism" is most associated with the literature and art of the 1920s. The fragmentation, dislocation, and disillusionment caused by World War I, especially in Europe, became a central theme of modernist writing—from James Joyce's *Ulysses* (1922), T.S. Eliot's *The Waste Land* (1922), and the novels of Virginia Woolf in Ireland and England to the works of "Lost Generation" expatriate Americans on the Continent—F. Scott Fitzgerald, Ernest Hemingway, E.E. Cummings, et al.—and the novels of William Faulkner in Mississippi.

Adams, Henry

(1838–1918)

A product of America's political and cultural elite, Henry Adams of Boston was an esteemed man of letters who eschewed his family's involvement in public service to pursue journalism and the study of history. The descendant of two presidents and a close friend of Theodore Roosevelt and William and Henry James, Adams was both a man of his time and deeply alienated from it. He is best known for his nine-volume *History of the United States During the Administrations of Thomas Jefferson and James Madison* (1889–1891) and his classic autobiography, *The Education of Henry Adams* (1918), an extended meditation on history, educational theory, and the social and cultural changes he witnessed during his lifetime.

Henry Brooks Adams was born in Boston on February 16, 1838, the grandson of President John Quincy Adams, the great-grandson of President John Adams, and the son of diplomat and historian Charles Francis Adams. After graduating from Harvard University in 1858, he spent two years traveling in Italy and France and studying law in Germany. From 1861 to 1868, he served as private secretary to his father, the U.S. minister to Great Britain during the critical years during and just after the Civil War. As an anonymous correspondent for *The New York Times,* the younger Adams came to believe that his greatest contribution to democratic ideals lay in journalism and scholarship. Ambivalent about his lineage, he came to feel that the values he inherited left him ineffectual and spiritually adrift amid the rise of industrial capitalism and decline of statesmanship during the Gilded Age.

Unwilling to make the sacrifices of principle needed to achieve success in politics or diplomacy, Adams spent much of his adult life in Washington, D.C., hoping to wield influence through his writing. Beginning with the Ulysses S. Grant administration, he urged civil service reform, retention of the silver standard, business regulation, and campaign finance reform in the prominent journals of the day. He continued his campaigns against political corruption and for government reform as editor of the respected *North American Review* from 1870 to 1876. Forays into fiction likewise reflected his disenchantment with contemporary politics and society. In his satirical political novel *Democracy* (1880, published anonymously), the protagonist confronts corruption and incompetence in Gilded Age Washington, D.C. Adams's next novel, *Esther* (1884, published under the pseudonym Frances Snow Compton), portrays his heroine's disillusionment with religion and marriage.

It was as a historian, however, that Adams attained his greatest eminence and most enduring influence. Appointed professor of medieval history at Harvard in 1870, he introduced the graduate seminar in U.S. higher education and collaborated with students in publishing *Essays in Anglo-Saxon Law* (1876), while also editing the *North American Review*. His extensive readings in contemporary social science led him to adapt the theories of Charles Darwin, John Stuart Mill, Herbert Spencer, and Karl Marx in formulating theoretical frameworks to explain developments in history.

Leaving Harvard in 1877, Adams moved with his wife, the former Marian "Clover" Hooper, to Washington, D.C., to devote himself to writing. Early works included the two novels and two historical biographies, the *Life of Albert Gallatin* (1879) and *John Randolph* (1882). His wife's suicide in 1885 led Adams to seek solace in work, travel, and the past. He engrossed himself in the monumental *History of the United States During the Administrations of Thomas Jefferson and James Madison,* which pioneered the use of archival and other primary sources as documentation, and followed the last volume of that work with a collection of political and economic treatises titled *Historical Essays* (1891).

While living part-time in France and immersing himself in its thirteenth-century cultural history, Adams wrote *Mont-Saint-Michel and Chartres* (printed privately, 1904; published 1918). At once travelogue and serious work of history, *Mont-Saint-Michel and Chartres* invokes the age of cathedrals as a time of spiritual and intellectual unity whose center was the veneration of the Virgin Mary. By way of counterpoint, *The Education of Henry Adams* (printed privately, 1907; published posthumously 1918) describes the multiplicity, confusion, and materialism wrought by modern science and technology. As against the unifying spiritual force of the medieval Virgin, Adams posits the modern Dynamo as a symbol of the dehumanizing energy of the modern mechanical world. *The Education of Henry Adams* was awarded the Pulitzer Prize for Biography or Autobiography in 1919.

Adams suffered a stroke in 1912, which limited his writing and traveling in the final years of his life. In a series of late essays, however, he sought to reconcile the study of history with modern advances in the physical sciences. Adams died at age 80 in Washington, D.C., on March 27, 1918.

Sue Barker

Chapter 35, "Nunc Age," *The Education of Henry Adams*, 1918

A landmark of American intellectual history, The Education of Henry Adams *is at once an introspective autobiography, treatise on the forces of historical change, and critical evaluation of the modern age. In the final chapter, "Nunc Age" ("Act Now"), Adams returns to New York after an extended trip to Europe and is overwhelmed—if not entirely pleased—by the size, power, and energy of the city. The progress has been frenetic and appears unstoppable, but Adams (who refers to himself in the third person) expresses hope for the future. As he and his contemporaries, such as diplomat John Hay, near their end, Adams expresses a wish to return on the centennial of his birth, 1938, and find a world that has learned from its mistakes—finally, he prays, "a world that sensitive and timid natures could regard without a shudder."*

Nearly forty years had passed since the ex-private secretary landed at New York with the ex-Ministers Adams and Motley, when they saw American society as a long caravan stretching out towards the plains. As he came up the bay again, November 5, 1904, an older man than either his father or Motley in 1868, he found the approach more striking than ever—wonderful—unlike anything man had ever seen—and like nothing he had ever much cared to see. The outline of the city became frantic in its effort to explain something that defied meaning. Power seemed to have outgrown its servitude and to have asserted its freedom. The cylinder had exploded, and thrown great masses of stone and steam against the sky. The city had the air and movement of hysteria, and the citizens were crying, in every accent of anger and alarm, that the new forces must at any cost be brought under control. Prosperity never before imagined, power never yet wielded by man, speed never reached by anything but a meteor, had made the world irritable, nervous, querulous, unreasonable and afraid. All New York was demanding new men, and all the new forces, condensed into corporations, were demanding a new type of man—a man with ten times the endurance, energy, will and mind of the old type—for whom they were ready to pay millions at sight. As one jolted over the pavements or read the last week's newspapers, the new man seemed close at hand, for the old one had plainly reached the end of his strength, and his failure had become catastrophic. Every one saw it, and every municipal election shrieked chaos. A traveller in the highways of history looked out of the club window on the turmoil of Fifth Avenue, and felt himself in Rome, under Diocletian, witnessing the anarchy, conscious of the compulsion, eager for the solution, but unable to conceive whence the next impulse was to come or how it was to act. The two-thousand-years failure of Christianity roared upward from Broadway, and no Constantine the Great was in sight.

Having nothing else to do, the traveller went on to Washington to wait the end. There Roosevelt was training Constantines and battling Trusts. With the Battle of Trusts, a student of mechanics felt entire sympathy, not merely as a matter of politics or society, but also as a measure of motion. The Trusts and Corporations stood for the larger part of the new power that had been created since 1840, and were obnoxious because of their vigorous and unscrupulous energy. They were revolutionary, troubling all the old conventions and values, as the screws of ocean steamers must

The city had the air and movement of hysteria, and the citizens were crying . . . that the new forces must at any cost be brought under control.

trouble a school of herring. They tore society to pieces and trampled it under foot. As one of their earliest victims, a citizen of Quincy, born in 1838, had learned submission and silence, for he knew that, under the laws of mechanics, any change, within the range of the forces, must make his situation only worse; but he was beyond measure curious to see whether the conflict of forces would produce the new man, since no other energies seemed left on earth to breed. The new man could be only a child born of contact between the new and the old energies.

Both had been familiar since childhood, as the story has shown, and neither had warped the umpire's judgment by its favors. If ever judge had reason to be impartial, it was he. The sole object of his interest and sympathy was the new man, and the longer one watched, the less could be seen of him. Of the forces behind the Trusts, one could see something; they owned a complete organization, with schools, training, wealth and purpose; but of the forces behind Roosevelt one knew little; their cohesion was slight; their training irregular; their objects vague. The public had no idea what practical system it could aim at, or what sort of men could manage it. The single problem before it was not so much to control the Trusts as to create the society that could manage the Trusts. The new American must be either the child of the new forces or a chance sport of nature. The attraction of mechanical power had already wrenched the American mind into a crab-like process which Roosevelt was making heroic efforts to restore to even action, and he had every right to active support and sympathy from all the world, especially from the Trusts themselves so far as they were human; but the doubt persisted whether the force that educated was really man or nature—mind or motion. The mechanical theory, mostly accepted by science, seemed to require that the law of mass should rule. In that case, progress would continue as before.

In that, or any other case, a nineteenth-century education was as useless or misleading as an eighteenth-century education had been to the child of 1838; but Adams had a better reason for holding his tongue. For his dynamic theory of history he cared no more than for the kinetic theory of gas; but, if it were an approach to measurement of motion, it would verify or disprove itself within thirty years. At the calculated acceleration, the head of the meteor-stream must very soon pass perihelion. Therefore, dispute was idle, discussion was futile, and silence, next to good-temper, was the mark of sense. If the acceleration, measured by the development and economy of forces, were to continue at its rate since 1800, the mathematician of 1950 should be able to plot the past and future orbit of the human race as accurately as that of the November meteoroids.

Naturally such an attitude annoyed the players in the game, as the attitude of the umpire is apt to infuriate the spectators. Above all, it was profoundly unmoral, and tended to discourage effort. On the other hand, it tended to encourage foresight and to economize waste of mind. If it was not itself education, it pointed out the economies necessary for the education of the new American. There, the duty stopped.

There, too, life stopped. Nature has educated herself to a singular sympathy for death. On the antarctic glacier, nearly five thousand feet above sea-level, Captain Scott found carcasses of seals, where the animals had laboriously flopped up, to die in peace. "Unless we had actually found these remains, it would have been past believing that a dying seal could have transported itself over fifty miles of rough, steep, glacier-surface," but "the seal seems often to crawl to the shore or the ice to die, probably from its instinctive dread of its marine enemies." In India, Purun Dass, at the end of statesmanship, sought solitude, and died in sanctity among the deer and monkeys, rather than remain with man. Even in America, the Indian Summer of life should be a little sunny and a little sad, like the season, and infinite in wealth and depth of tone—but never hustled. For that reason, one's own passive obscurity seemed sometimes nearer nature than John Hay's exposure. To the normal animal the instinct of sport is innate, and historians themselves were not exempt from the passion of baiting their bears; but in its turn even the seal dislikes to be worried to death in age by creatures that have not the strength or the teeth to kill him outright.

On reaching Washington, November 14, 1904, Adams saw at a glance that Hay must have rest. Already Mrs. Hay had bade him prepare to help in taking her husband to Europe as soon as the Session should be over, and although Hay protested that the idea could not even be discussed, his strength failed so rapidly that he could not effectually discuss it, and ended by yielding without struggle. He would equally have resigned office and retired, like Purun Dass, had not the President and the press protested; but he often debated the subject, and his friends could throw no light on it. Adams himself, who had set his heart on seeing Hay close his career by making peace in the East, could only urge that vanity for vanity, the crown of peacemaker was worth the cross of martyrdom; but the cross was full in sight, while the crown was still uncertain. Adams found his formula for Russian inertia exasperatingly correct. He thought that Russia should have negotiated instantly on the fall of Port Arthur, January 1, 1905; he found that she had not the energy, but meant to wait till her navy should be destroyed. The delay measured precisely the time that Hay had to spare.

The close of the Session on March 4 left him barely the strength to crawl on board ship, March 18, and before his steamer had reached half her course, he had revived, almost as gay as when he first lighted on the Markoe house in I Street forty-four years earlier. The clouds that gather round the setting sun do not always take a sober coloring from eyes that have kept watch on mortality; or, at least, the sobriety is sometimes scarcely sad. One walks with one's friends squarely up to the portal of life, and bids good-bye with a smile. One has done it so often! Hay could scarcely pace the deck; he nourished no illusions; he was convinced that he should never return to his work, and he talked lightly of the death sentence that he might any day expect, but he threw off the coloring of office and mortality together, and the malaria of power left its only trace in the sense of tasks incomplete.

One could honestly help him there. Laughing frankly at his dozen treaties hung up in the Senate Committee-room like lambs in a butcher's shop, one could still remind him of what was solidly completed. In his eight years of office he had solved nearly every old problem of American statesmanship, and had left little or nothing to annoy his successor. He had brought the great Atlantic powers into a working system, and even Russia seemed about to be dragged into a combine of intelligent equilibrium based on an intelligent allotment of activities. For the first time in fifteen hundred years a true Roman *pax* was in sight, and would, if it succeeded, owe its virtues to him. Except for making peace in Manchuria, he could do no more; and if the worst should happen, setting continent against continent in arms—the only apparent alternative to his scheme—he need not repine at missing the catastrophe.

This rosy view served to soothe disgusts which every parting statesman feels, and commonly with reason. One had no need to get out one's notebook in order to jot down the exact figures on either side. Why add up the elements of resistance and anarchy? The Kaiser supplied him with these figures, just as the Cretic approached Morocco. Every one was doing it, and seemed in a panic about it. The chaos waited only for his landing.

Arrived at Genoa, the party hid itself for a fortnight at Nervi, and he gained strength rapidly as long as he made no effort and heard no call for action. Then they all went on to Nanheim without relapse. There, after a few days, Adams left him for the regular treatment, and came up to Paris. The medical reports promised well, and Hay's letters were as humorous and light-handed as ever. To the last he wrote cheerfully of his progress, and amusingly with his usual light scepticism, of his various doctors; but when the treatment ended, three weeks later, and he came on to Paris, he showed, at the first glance, that he had lost strength, and the return to affairs and interviews wore him rapidly out. He was conscious of it, and in his last talk before starting for London and Liverpool he took the end of his activity for granted. "You must hold out for the peace negotiations," was the remonstrance. "I've not time!" he replied. "You'll need little time!" was the rejoinder. Each was correct.

There it ended! Shakespeare himself could use no more than the commonplace to express what is incapable of expression. "The rest is silence!" The few familiar words, among the simplest in the language, conveying an idea trite beyond rivalry, served Shakespeare, and, as yet, no one has said more. A few weeks afterwards, one warm evening in early July, as Adams was strolling down to dine under the trees at Armenonville, he learned that Hay was dead. He expected it; on Hay's account, he was even satisfied to have his friend die, as we would all die if we could, in full fame, at home and abroad, universally regretted, and wielding his power to the last. One had seen scores of emperors and heroes fade into cheap obscurity even when alive; and now, at least, one had not that to fear for one's friend. It was not even the suddenness of the shock, or the sense of void, that threw Adams into the depths of Hamlet's Shakespearean silence in the full flare of Paris frivolity in its favorite haunt where worldly vanity reached its most futile climax in human history; it was only the quiet summons to follow—the assent to dismissal. It was time to go. The three friends had begun life together; and the last of the three had no motive—no attraction—to carry it on after the others had gone. Education had ended for all three, and only beyond some remoter horizon could its values be fixed or renewed. Perhaps some day—say 1938, their centenary—they might be allowed to return together for a holiday, to see the mistakes of their own lives made clear in the light of the mistakes of their successors; and perhaps then, for the first time since man began his education among the carnivores, they would find a world that sensitive and timid natures could regard without a shudder.

Sources: Bartleby.com (www.bartleby.com); Henry Adams, *The Education of Henry Adams* (Boston: Houghton Mifflin, 1918).

Alger, Horatio
(1832–1899)

Known as the father of "rags-to-riches" tales, Horatio Alger was the author of up to 135 dime novels for boys that helped perpetuate the "myth of the self-made man" and the Protestant work ethic in modern industrial America. Typically set in one of the urban centers that developed with the rise of industrialism in the post–Civil War era, his stories inevitably recount the struggles of an honest, enterprising boy who overcomes adversity to achieve success and respectability. Formulaic in plot, easy to read, and ever optimistic in outlook, Alger's books made him one of America's most popular writers from the 1870s to 1890s. Sales soared even higher in the early twentieth century, after his death, thanks to the propaganda value of his stories to socially conservative Americans who opposed Progressive Era reforms. Then and thereafter, his characters were touted as embodiments of the "American Dream," "rugged individualism," and "lifting oneself up by the bootstraps."

Alger's own life story did not exactly follow the moral-uplift formula of his books. Born in Revere, Massachusetts, on January 13, 1832, he was raised in a home that cherished education and religion. A Phi Beta Kappa graduate of Harvard Divinity School (1852), he originally hoped to become a poet but took a position as a correspondent for the New York *Sun*. Unable to serve in the Civil War due to asthma, he spent a year of soul-searching in Paris and returned to follow in his father's footsteps and become a Unitarian minister. Ordained in 1864, he was installed as a pastor in Brewster, Massachusetts, but resigned two years later amid allegations of sexual misconduct with boys. In 1866, he moved to New York City to establish himself as a professional writer for young adults.

Fascinated by the poor and orphaned "ragged boys" of New York's ghettos, Alger began writing the books—beginning with *Ragged Dick; or, Street Life in New York* in 1868—that grew into his popular

Horatio Alger's formulaic rags-to-riches stories for teenage boys reinforced the American Dream—upward mobility through honesty and hard work—in modern industrial society.

six-volume Ragged Dick series. The character of Ragged Dick, as well as counterparts in the Luck and Pluck series (from 1869) and Tattered Tom series (from 1871), is a disadvantaged street boy who achieves upward mobility through honesty and hard work. In that regard, his books reflect the class tensions apparent in Alger's time, as well as the moral tensions in his private life.

Alger's stories typically begin with the hero's performance of a daring deed, such as rescuing the daughter of a prominent citizen from injury or death. The grateful father becomes the boy's bene-factor, bestowing gifts and, more important, an opportunity for advancement through pluck and diligence. Seizing the chance, the young man is saved from ruin and becomes a respected member of the community, and sometimes rich to boot. As some critics have noted, however, the final reward—social standing, honor, wealth, or all of these—is not always strictly earned. Sheer luck often plays a role, as does the intervention of an unexpected benefactor.

Alger lived for 30 years in New York City, where he wrote most of his books and worked on behalf of homeless children. He died of lung and heart ailments at his sister's home in South Natick, Massachusetts, on July 18, 1899. His books have sold more than 20 million copies.

Jennifer Harrison

"Tom Parker's Strange Visitor," 1892

Except for the fact that it takes place in an Iowa farm town rather than a large industrial city, Horatio Alger's late short story "Tom Parker's Strange Visitor" reflects the essential themes, plot elements, and protagonist character traits for which his classic rags-to-riches tales are known: a virtuous teenage boy who overcomes evil and earns just rewards, however unexpected, for his ingenuity and moxie. The story originally appeared in the December 17, 1892, edition of Argosy *magazine.*

"Somehow, Hannah, I feel rather skittish about leaving home tonight. I've got a—what do you call it—presentiment that something will happen while I am gone."

"What can happen, Reuben? You know Tom will be here."

"I'll tell you a secret, Hannah. In my desk yonder there is a wallet containing five hundred dollars."

"Where on earth did you get so much money, Reuben?" asked Mrs. Parker in great surprise.

"I will tell you. When Joe Bent went to California two years since, I lent him a hundred and twenty five dollars. Yesterday I received by Wells and Fargo's express the sum of five hundred dollars, of which I am to keep one hundred and fifty for my loan and interest, and the balance Joe wants me to put into some savings bank for him. I mean to go to Castleton tomorrow and carry the money with me, but tonight I must keep it here."

"I don't see how there can be any danger, Reuben. No one knows that the money is in the house."

"We can't tell. When the express package was handed to me there were two persons present—strangers to me. They might have suspected what the bundle contained."

"If you feel anxious, Reuben, we can stay at home."

"No; Lucy would be disappointed. She expects me to be present at the christening of our grandchild, and there is no reason which I could venture to give for staying away. We will go, and trust to good luck that no harm comes of it."

"Better tell Tom, so as to put him on his guard."

Reuben Parker was a farmer and lived in Northern Iowa. His farm was a large one, and was distant a mile and a half from the village of Horton, in whose town limits it was located.

Though somewhat isolated, the farmer's family never felt any fears of injury from wandering tramps or thieves, chiefly because it was seldom that anything likely to attract their cupidity was to be found in the house. Tonight, however, for the first time, a presentiment of evil disturbed the farmer's peace of mind. Yet he felt that he could not well break the engagement to spend the evening at his daughter's house in Castleton, five miles away.

"After all," he said to himself, "why need I borrow trouble? Tom will stay and mind the house, and there is little chance that any one knows about the money. I won't be foolish, but go prepared to have a good time. But I must first have a talk with Tom."

Tom Parker was the farmer's only son, six years younger than his married sister, and a strong, sturdy, manly boy of sixteen. There was nothing delicate or dude-like about him. He was a boy to be proud of.

In a few words Reuben Parker explained the situation to his son.

"Now, Tom," he concluded, "are you afraid to be left in charge of this money?"

"No, father, why should I be? Do you think these is any chance of any one knowing there is money in the house?"

"Very little, but professional thieves make it their business to find out such things."

"Is there any one you particularly suspect?"

"I have heard that Steve Berry, the notorious outlaw, has been seen in Castleton lately, and if so he is no doubt intent upon some evil scheme. Still, I can't understand how he should know anything of the money in my desk."

"What is his appearance, father?"

"He is a tall, heavily built man, with short black whiskers, and a scar on the left cheek."

"Then if he calls I shall know him," said Tom, smiling.

"He needs to be cautious, for there is a reward of five hundred dollars offered for his apprehension."

"I should think he would leave the State."

"He is bold, and no one ever charged him with lack of courage. Some time he will prove too bold and will be caught."

"I should like to be the one to catch him and receive the reward."

"Yes, five hundred dollars would come handy to any of us. Well, Tom, good night. The buggy is at the door and it is time to start."

"When will you be back, father?"

"Probably by eleven o'clock."

"Then I hope Steve Berry will postpone his call till that time."

"Yes; if he comes while I am here I will be ready for him."

The farmer helped his wife into the buggy and the horse started briskly in the direction of Castleton.

"Well," thought Tom, as he settled himself in the rocking chair before the fire, "I am in for a lonely evening, I suppose. It is not yet seven, and the folks won't get back till eleven at least. What shall I do to fill up the time?"

After a little consideration Tom came to a decision. Though his educational advantages had been limited, he was fond of study, and particularly of mathematics. In arithmetic he had ciphered as far as cube root, and had begun algebra. This last he liked, but he had been obliged to give it up, as the last teacher whose school he had attended didn't understand it.

Tom had made a beginning, however, and having the book at home he had gone on, as well as he could, in his leisure hours without assistance. It struck him that the long evening before him could not be better employed than in trying to solve some of the problems that had puzzled him.

He drew up a small table in front of his chair, and taking from his father's desk a sheet of foolscap, tackled a problem which thus far had baffled him.

Time passes quickly when a boy is studying, as many of my young readers can testify, and probably Tom had been occupied for an hour when he was startled by a knock at the front door. The farmhouse was not provided with that modem improvement, a door bell.

I said Tom was startled, and this was true. Callers in the evening, so isolated was the farmhouse, were rare, and this evening in particular, when all except himself were away, there seemed less chance than usual of any interruption from visitors.

"Who can it be?" thought Tom, as he laid his algebra down on the table.

He didn't immediately go to the door, and the visitor, whoever he might be, became impatient, for another knock, louder and more imperative than the first, woke the echoes in the old house.

"I must go and see who it is," thought Tom.

He opened the front door, holding the light. A strong gust of wind nearly blew it out, but Tom shielded it with his hand and looked curiously at the visitor.

His heart beat in quick excitement, not unmingled with dismay, when he found him to be *a tall, heavily, built man, with short black whiskers, and a scar on the left cheek!*

Could it be the notorious Steve Berry of whom his father had spoken? Yes, it must be. The resemblance was perfect.

"Well, kid," said the caller impatiently, "what are you staring at? Are you struck dumb?"

"What can I do for you?" asked Tom, recovering his wits.

"You can invite me in out of the cold," said the visitor. "I suppose you have a fire?"

"Yes, sir," answered Tom.

"Well, lead the way in, and I will follow."

Tom did as he was told—there seemed no other way—and Steve Berry followed him into the cozy sitting room.

"Ah, that's something like," said the visitor as he drew a chair up to the open log fire and spread out his hands before it. "Do you know, kid, it's growing cold fast?"

"I suppose it is," answered Tom.

"You seem to be alone," went on Berry, casting a glower around the room.

"Yes, my father and mother have gone out to make a call."

"And won't be home till late in the evening."

"How can he know that?" Tom asked himself, startled.

"It's quite a distance to Castleton," continued Berry composedly.

"How do you know they have gone there?" asked Tom.

"I saw them entering the village," answered Berry, "and it occurred to me that you might be lonely, so I just plodded on to spend the evening with you. I nearly repented of my bargain, though, when I found how cold it was."

"I wish you had given it up," thought Tom.

Looking about with his quick, keen glance Berry noticed the algebra.

"What's that?" he asked.

"An algebra."

"And were you amusing yourself with it when I came?"

"I was trying to solve a problem, but it puzzled me."

"Show it to me."

In great surprise Tom handed over the book and pointed out the sum which had perplexed him.

"I used to be pretty good in algebra," said Berry. "Give me a piece of paper."

Tom handed him the paper on which he had been figuring.

"Is that your work?"

"Yes."

Steve Berry looked it over.

"I'll show you your mistake," he said, "and I'll show you the correct way of solving the problem. Draw your chair up to mine."

Tom did so, and in a few words the visitor made the matter clear.

"Do you understand now?" asked Berry.

"Yes, thank you. What a talent you have for mathematics!"

Berry laughed, but he was evidently pleased.

"Yes," he said, "I ought to have been a professor of mathematics. As it is—by the way," and he bent a keen glance into Tom's face, "do you know who I am?"

"I think you are Steve Berry," answered Tom, after a slight hesitation.

"You've got it right the first time, kid. And what am I? Come, let it out! Don't be bashful!"

"I think you are a—burglar."

"Right. I am glad you understand me. It will save trouble. I may as well come to business. In that desk yonder is a package of money. Go and get it. I want it."

The crisis had come, and Tom felt that he was unprepared for it.

"Mr. Berry," he said in agitation, "that money doesn't belong to us—at any rate, only a part of it. Don't take it!"

"My boy, I am sorry to disappoint you, but I can't let any one interfere with my business. I have come here expressly for that money, and I must have it."

"Then take it yourself. I won't give it to you."

"All right!"

Steve Berry rose, went over to the desk, and searching it, soon found the roll of bills. He counted them over with a face indicating satisfaction, and said aloud—Good! here's five hundred dollars."

"Only one hundred and fifty belongs to my father," said Tom. "Take that, and leave the rest."

"That would be very unbusinesslike, and I can't consent. I need it, and, besides, I think I deserve some pay for the help I gave you with your algebra."

Poor Tom! He was in despair, but he was no match for the burly robber, and he knew not what to do.

Steve Berry became quite lively and jovial.

"Come, boy," he said, "I feel like making a night of it. Haven't you got any whisky in the house?"

"We have some cider."

"Well, get that."

Tom rose to comply with Berry's request, and there flashed into his mind a way to recover the money. He went into the adjoining room, used as a kitchen, and in the closet he found a jug of cider.

On the second shelf was a flask filled with a fine white powder which his mother had used as a sleeping potion in a recent sickness. Quickly Tom poured the whole contents of the flask into the jug of cider, and then taking the latter into the sitting room, set it on the table with a glass.

"Help yourself, Mr. Berry," he said.

Steve Berry did so, nothing loath.

He drained a glass at a draught.

"Ah!" he said, smacking his lips, "that reminds me of my boyhood days. Take a glass, kid."

"Cider don't agree with me," answered Tom.

"I am sorry to drink alone, but that cider is good. I'm not afraid of it."

He poured out two glasses more and drained them.

Then he drew up a lounge and lay down just opposite the fire.

Tom watched him in feverish excitement. Soon the potion began to work. Berry's eyes closed and his breathing became deep and regular. Presently he seemed to be in a profound slumber.

Then Tom, his heart beating quickly, prepared to act.

He approached the sleeping man, and from his side pocket gently withdrew the wallet containing the bills. He paused two or three times to make sure that he was still unconscious.

He put the wallet in his own pocket, and then opening the outer door stole quietly from the house.

How he ever got over the five miles between the farmhouse and Castleton he hardly knew. But he came panting and excited into his sister's house, and as soon as he could he told his story.

"And you left Steve Berry asleep in the sitting room?" asked his father.

"Yes."

"We will go home at once."

Reuben Parker and two officers from Castleton set out at once and went as fast as their horses could carry them to the farm.

They found all as Tom had represented. Steve Berry was fast asleep on the lounge, and the fire was burning brightly. They had little difficulty in binding the sleeping burglar. When he came to himself he was a captive.

"What is all this?" he asked.

"What sent me to sleep?"

"The cider was drugged," answered Reuben Parker.

"And the boy did it?"

"Yes."

"You're a smart one, kid!" said the burglar. "You're the first one, boy or man, that has fooled Steve Berry. Well, I won't bear a grudge. I would have done the same in your case."

Steve Berry was tried, convicted and sentenced to a term of imprisonment. The five hundred dollars which had been offered as a reward for his apprehension were given to Tom Parker, who feels well repaid for his long and lonely walk to Castleton. He still keeps up his algebra, but expects no more assistance from Steve Berry.

Source: Horatio Alger Digital Serials Project, Northern Illinois University Libraries (www.ulib.niu.edu).

Anderson, Sherwood

(1876–1941)

The Ohio-born novelist and short-story writer Sherwood Anderson is best known for naturalistic works of fiction that captured small-town Midwestern life in simple yet elegant prose. His many novels and collections—the best known of which is the short-story sequence *Winesburg, Ohio* (1919)—chronicle the difficult and painful period of transition to modernity in preindustrial small-town America. Dramatizing the tensions between instinctive human nature and the inhibitions and isolation imposed by conventional industrial society, *Winesburg* was one of the first works of fiction directly influenced by psychoanalytic theory and is recognized as one of the seminal works of the modernist movement in American literature. William Faulkner, one of a number of younger novelists who acknowledged a debt to Anderson's prose style, called him "the father of my generation of American writers and the tradition of American writing which our successors will carry on."

Sherwood Anderson was born in Camden, Ohio, on September 13, 1876, the son of a saddle and harness maker. He spent his childhood in Clyde, a town in the north-central part of the state that would later inspire the stories in *Winesburg*. After an upbringing that included only sporadic formal schooling and work as a housepainter, stable hand, and newsboy, he served in Cuba during the Spanish-American War in 1898.

Returning to the United States, Anderson briefly attended Wittenberg Academy in Springfield, Ohio, then managed a paint factory in Elyria and married and started a family. In 1912, however, following an emotional breakdown, he turned his back on both his "materialistic existence" and his family and moved to Chicago, where he found work as an advertising copywriter. Through his brother, he met a circle of writers known as the Chicago Group, which included Carl Sandburg and Theodore Dreiser, who encouraged him to pursue his writing seriously.

Anderson's first published work, the autobiographical novel *Windy McPherson's Son*, appeared in 1916, followed by *Marching Men* (1917), a novel about the plight of coal miners in eastern Pennsylvania, and then a series of prose poems titled *Mid-American Chants* (1918). Upon publication in 1919, *Winesburg, Ohio* won critical acclaim—the respected H.L. Mencken said it contained "some of the most remarkable writing done in America in our time"—and established a national reputation for its author.

Despite its bucolic setting, the book was regarded as revolutionary in both theme and style. Made up of 24 interwoven sketches and short stories, and written in the simple style of everyday speech, *Winesburg* explores the inner "truths" and conflicts of the citizens of a small Midwestern town. Yet Anderson's character-driven fiction reaches beyond psychological portraiture, containing a heavy strain of social commentary as well. Many of the characters in *Winesburg* and his other works find themselves painfully at odds with prevailing cultural ideals concerning material success and the American Dream—ideals that too often prove false and unattainable. In the 1920 novel *Poor White*, Anderson examines the harmful effects of rapid industrialization on a Midwestern farm town, pitting the quest for financial success against the destruction of a traditional community. And in *Dark Laughter* (1925), in which the protagonist retraces Mark Twain's travels on the Mississippi River, Anderson continues to explore the dissonance between the promise of nineteenth-century America and the grim realities of an increasingly urban and industrialized nation.

Anderson moved repeatedly after the success of *Winesburg* and was married a total of four times. He wrote for magazines in New York City in 1921 and then moved to Paris, where he joined the literary salon of Gertrude Stein. Returning to the United States the following year, he settled in New Orleans, where he befriended Faulkner and other writers and editors associated with an avant-garde "little magazine" called the *Double Dealer*. In 1925, he purchased a farm in southwestern Virginia, where he began editing two weekly newspapers. Anderson traveled extensively for the rest of his life and died on March 8, 1941, after swallowing a toothpick and developing peritonitis on a trip to South America to write about labor conditions.

Rod Phillips

See also: Literature of the Gilded Age and Progressive Era—*Sidelight:* Modern and Modernism; Naturalism

◇◇

"The Book of the Grotesque," *Winesburg, Ohio,* 1919

◇◇

In radical contrast to the plot-driven, moralistic fiction in vogue at the time, Sherwood Anderson's naturalistic, psychologically complex portrayals of small-town inhabitants—or "grotesques," as he called them—were the central focus of the connected short stories that make up Winesburg, Ohio. *The opening chapter, "The Book of the Grotesque," serves as a prologue to the 24 stories that follow, each about one of the odd, somehow distorted residents of the town. As Anderson later wrote, this idiosyncratic opening sketch—about a lonely unnamed old writer who begins envisioning people he has known as grotesques—came to him all at once as he lay in bed one night in Chicago. He went to his typewriter and finished the piece in one sitting. "The rest of the book came out of me on succeeding evenings," Anderson would recount, "and sometimes during the day while I worked in the advertising office."*

The writer, an old man with a white mustache, had some difficulty in getting into bed. The windows of the house in which he lived were high and he wanted to look at the trees when he awoke in the morning. A carpenter came to fix the bed so that it would be on a level with the window.

Quite a fuss was made about the matter. The carpenter, who had been a soldier in the Civil War, came into the writer's room and sat down to talk of building a platform for the purpose of raising the bed. The writer had cigars lying about and the carpenter smoked.

For a time the two men talked of the raising of the bed and then they talked of other things. The soldier got on the subject of the war. The writer, in fact, led him to that subject. The carpenter had once been a prisoner in Andersonville prison and had lost a brother. The brother had died of starvation, and whenever the carpenter got upon that subject he cried. He, like the old writer, had a white mustache, and when he cried he puckered up his lips and the mustache bobbed up and down. The weeping old man with the cigar in his mouth was ludicrous. The plan the writer had for the raising of his bed was forgotten and later the carpenter did it in his own way and the writer, who was past sixty, had to help himself with a chair when he went to bed at night.

In his bed the writer rolled over on his side and lay quite still. For years he had been beset with notions concerning his heart. He was a hard smoker and his heart fluttered. The idea had got into his mind that he would some time die unexpectedly and always when he got into bed he thought of that. It did not alarm him. The effect in fact was quite a special thing and not easily explained. It made him more alive, there in bed, than at any other time. Perfectly still he lay and his body was old and not of much use any more, but something inside him was altogether young. He was like a pregnant woman, only that the thing inside him was not a baby but a youth. No, it wasn't a youth, it was a woman, young, and wearing a coat of mail like a knight. It is absurd, you see, to try to tell what was inside the old writer as he lay on his high bed and listened to the fluttering of his heart. The thing to get at is what the writer, or the young thing within the writer, was thinking about.

The old writer, like all of the people in the world, had got, during his long fife, a great many notions in his head. He had once been quite handsome and a number of women had been in love with him. And then, of course, he had known people, many people, known them in a peculiarly intimate way that was different from the way in which you and I know people. At least that is what the writer thought and the thought pleased him. Why quarrel with an old man concerning his thoughts?

In the bed the writer had a dream that was not a dream. As he grew somewhat sleepy but was still conscious, figures began to appear before his eyes. He imagined the young indescribable thing within himself was driving a long procession of figures before his eyes.

You see the interest in all this lies in the figures that went before the eyes of the writer. They were all grotesques. All of the men and women the writer had ever known had become grotesques.

The grotesques were not all horrible. Some were amusing, some almost beautiful, and one, a woman all drawn out of shape, hurt the old man by her grotesqueness. When she passed he made a noise like a small dog whimpering. Had you come into the room you might have supposed the old man had unpleasant dreams or perhaps indigestion.

For an hour the procession of grotesques passed before the eyes of the old man, and then, although it was a painful thing to do, he crept out of bed and began to write. Some one of the grotesques had made a deep impression on his mind and he wanted to describe it.

At his desk the writer worked for an hour. In the end he wrote a book which he called "The Book of the Grotesque." It was never published, but I saw it once and it made an indelible impression on my mind. The book had one central thought that is very strange and has always remained with me. By remembering it I have been able to understand many people and things that I was never able to understand before. The thought was involved but a simple statement of it would be something like this:

That in the beginning when the world was young there were a great many thoughts but no such thing as a truth. Man made the truths himself and each truth was a composite of a great many vague thoughts. All about in the world were the truths and they were all beautiful.

The old man had listed hundreds of the truths in his book. I will not try to tell you of all of them. There was the truth of virginity and the truth of passion, the truth of wealth and of poverty, of thrift and of profligacy, of carelessness and abandon. Hundreds and hundreds were the truths and they were all beautiful.

And then the people came along. Each as he appeared snatched up one of the truths and some who were quite strong snatched up a dozen of them.

It was the truths that made the people grotesques. The old man had quite an elaborate theory concerning the matter. It was his notion that the moment one of the people took one of the truths to himself, called it his truth, and tried to live his life by it, he became a grotesque and the truth he embraced became a falsehood.

You can see for yourself how the old man, who had spent all of his life writing and was filled with words, would write hundreds of pages concerning this matter. The subject would become so big in his mind that he himself would be in danger of becoming a grotesque. He didn't, I suppose, for the same reason that he never published the book. It was the young thing inside him that saved the old man.

Concerning the old carpenter who fixed the bed for the writer, I only mentioned him because he, like many of what are called very common people, became the nearest thing to what is understandable and lovable of all the grotesques in the writer's book.

Sources: Bartleby.com (www.bartleby.com/159); Sherwood Anderson, *Winesburg, Ohio* (New York: B.W. Huebsch, 1919).

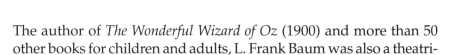

Baum, L. Frank

(1856–1919)

The author of *The Wonderful Wizard of Oz* (1900) and more than 50 other books for children and adults, L. Frank Baum was also a theatrical and motion picture producer, a journalist, and an expert on topics ranging from retail show windows to raising purebred chickens.

Born on May 15, 1856, to a wealthy family near Syracuse, New York, Lyman Frank Baum began making up stories and writing as a child, as a weak heart kept him from more active pursuits. Home-schooled, he spent hours reading in his father's library, daydreaming, and producing an amateur newspaper with his brother on a cheap home printing press. In his early twenties, after stints in the family business and breeding poultry, Baum became enamored with the stage and wrote and produced plays at a theater his father built for him in Richburg, New York, in 1880. One of his productions, *The Maid of Arran*, proved moderately successful, and Baum toured the country for the next two years in a starring role. While he was away, the theater in Richburg burned down.

In November 1882, Baum married Maud Gage, a daughter of the famous suffragist Matilda Joslyn Gage. When Maud became pregnant, Baum left the stage and returned to Syracuse to work again in the family business. In 1888, the collapse of his father's fortune led Baum to follow his wife's brother and sister to Aberdeen, South Dakota, where he opened a novelty store. Forced to close the shop after just 15 months because of financial difficulties, Baum spent the next year editing the *Aberdeen Saturday Pioneer*. This helped him support the local Republican Party and women's rights as well as his family; he and his wife also became adherents of the theosophical spiritual movement.

By 1891, drought and crop failures in Aberdeen prompted Baum to move the family to Chicago, where he worked as a traveling sales-man and began writing children's books. His first published work,

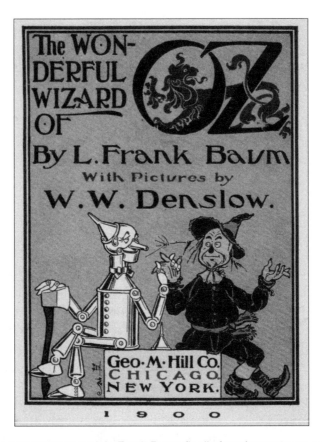

Footloose and multitalented, L. Frank Baum finally found success as a children's writer with *The Wonderful Wizard of Oz* (1900). The bestselling novel spawned 13 sequels, a stage musical, and, of course, the 1939 film favorite.

Mother Goose in Prose, illustrated by Maxfield Parrish, was greeted in 1897 with strong reviews but modest sales. More successful was his new periodical, *Show Window,* the first trade journal in America for window dressers. But Baum was intent on becoming a children's writer, and his 1899 collaboration with illustrator W.W. Denslow, *Father Goose: His Book,* became a best seller. The following year, Baum and Denslow worked together again to produce the iconic children's novel, *The Wonderful Wizard of Oz.*

Baum incorporated many of his own life experiences in the fantasy world of Oz. He transformed the harsh, drought-stricken South Dakota landscape into Dorothy's Kansas. The dramatic color and costumes in the book reflected his training in the theater and window display design; his feminist politics were embodied in the story's strong female protagonist. Above all, Baum's imagination and humor, along with his uniquely American interpretation of the fairy-tale genre, made the book appealing to generations of adults as well as children. A 1902 musical theater adaptation was at least as popular as the book and toured the country for nearly a decade. The 1939 motion picture version, with Judy Garland starring as Dorothy, remains one of the most popular films in Hollywood history.

Wealthy almost instantly, Baum and his family moved to Pasadena, California, where he wrote 13 sequels to *The Wonderful Wizard* up until his death; among them are *The Marvelous Land of Oz* (1904), *The Emerald City of Oz* (1909), *Tik-Tok Man of Oz* (1914), and *The Scarecrow of Oz* (1915). A succession of business setbacks, including a failed motion picture company, and medical expenses compelled Baum to produce dozens of other books, including six for boys under the pen name Floyd Akers and 24 for girls under the pseudonym Edith Van Dyne. He died of a stroke on May 6, 1919, in Hollywood.

Paul B. Ringel

Sidelight

Political Interpretations of *The Wizard of Oz*

Celebrated as an American cultural icon, L. Frank Baum's *The Wonderful Wizard of Oz* has been a source of fascination to generations of scholars. Some have interpreted the story as a political or religious allegory, others as a vision of American utopia, still others as a tribute to consumer capitalism. Treatments of the text as a turn-of-the-century political allegory began with an article in the spring 1964 issue of *American Quarterly* titled "The Wizard of Oz: Parable on Populism," by a high school history teacher named Henry Littlefield. The article touched off ongoing debate and speculation among cultural critics as to the political symbolism of Baum's great American fairy tale.

The Wizard, in Littlefield's view, "reflects to an astonishing degree the world of political reality which surrounded Baum in 1900." Central to that reality were Western farmer-Populists, like those Baum met during his years in South Dakota, who wanted the government to print more money so they could pay off their farm debts with "cheaper" dollars and sell their crops at higher prices. In the wake of the Panic of 1893 and the three-year economic depression that followed, Americans were deeply divided over the nation's monetary policy. The financial establishment of the Northeast favored the deflationary gold standard, which limited the money supply. "Silverites," or proponents of the "free-silver" policy, called for the use of both silver and gold (at a ratio of 16:1) as the basis of the currency. The latter approach, everyone agreed, would raise prices. For the Populist movement of the 1890s, based in the agrarian Great Plains, free silver was a core tenet and an essential weapon in the fight against economic oppression at the hands of bankers, railroads, and robber barons.

The visual imagery and story line of *The Wizard of Oz*, say Henry Littlefield and other critics, allude to these issues with compelling consistency. Dorothy, says Littlefield, is "Baum's Miss Everyman," a simple, Populist character from the heartland (Kansas) and a personification of American values. The tornado that sweeps her away can be understood as a catastrophic or transformational event, such as the Panic of 1893 or the free-silver movement that swept the Midwest. Dorothy is carried off to the Land of Oz, whose name derives from the standard measure of the gold ounce; hence, Oz may be equated with the United States at the time, a land where the gold standard held sway. So Dorothy heads out on the Yellow Brick Road—the route of gold—in search of home. Importantly, she wears silver slippers (changed to ruby slippers in the film version), symbols of her belief in free silver and its promise of salvation.

The path of gold, of course, leads to the Emerald City—the "capital" of Oz and a symbol of the illusory world in which greenbacks (paper money) only appear to have value. At the center of the domain is the "man behind the curtain," a politi-cian-like charlatan who operates devices to fool the people into believing that he is great, powerful, and benevolent when he is, in fact, feckless. Extending the metaphor, as some scholars certainly have, the character of the Scarecrow may symbolize the troubled Western farmer; the Tin Woodman (or Tin Man) can stand for the industrial worker, a wood chopper whose entire body has been replaced by metal parts (dehumanized by machinery); and the Cowardly Lion is said to represent William Jennings Bryan, a leading Populist politician and orator (known for his "roar" but criticized by some as fainthearted for failing to support the U.S. war with Spain in 1898).

If Baum's political allegory is so complete and consistent, what was his true purpose in writing *The Wonderful Wizard of Oz?* To entertain readers or to comment on politics? Whatever his satirical impulses, Baum was clear that his motivation was to enchant young readers. As he stated in the introduction to the 1900 edition, he wrote the book "solely to pleasure children of today." Even Henry Littlefield could not suspect a higher motive. "*The Wizard* has become a genuine piece of American folklore," he wrote in his 1964 article, "because, knowing his audience, Baum never allowed the consistency of the allegory to take precedence over the theme of youthful entertainment."

Bierce, Ambrose

(1842–1914?)

Ambrose Bierce was a short-story writer, journalist, and critic famous for his scathing wit, grim humor, and contributions to American realism during the era of Western expansion following the Civil War. As a star reporter and editorialist for William Randolph Hearst's San Francisco *Examiner* beginning in the late 1880s, Bierce was a notorious cynic and pessimist who excoriated virtually every important institution in the country and voiced strong opinions on everything from political corruption and U.S. military action to the works of fellow writers. Today he is best remembered for his short stories, which gave a Western setting to Gothic fiction, and for a collection of satirical definitions titled *The Devil's Dictionary* (1911). Bierce's disappearance in December 1913 while reporting on the Mexican Revolution remains one of the great unsolved mysteries in American literary history.

The tenth of 13 children (all of whose first names began with "A"), Ambrose Gwinnett Bierce was born on June 24, 1842, into a poor, religiously devout farming family in Horse Cave, Ohio. Raised in Kosciusko County, Indiana, he read extensively in his father's farmhouse library but had only a smattering of formal education before leaving home at age 15 to become a printer's apprentice.

At age 19, at the outset of the Civil War, Bierce enlisted in the Union Army. His experiences in battle—he participated in some of the most horrific fighting at Shiloh (1862) and Chickamauga (1863) and suffered a serious head injury at Kennesaw Mountain (1864)—left their mark on the psyche of the man who would earn the nickname "Bitter Bierce." Many years later, Bierce drew on his wartime experiences in *Tales of Soldiers and Civilians* (1891), which included the celebrated ghost story "Occurrence at Owl Creek Bridge." Many critics came to regard Bierce's *Tales* alongside Stephen Crane's *Red Badge of Courage* (1895) as the pinnacle of American Civil War fiction.

Traveling west in 1866, Bierce served as a civilian engineer on an expedition to inspect military outposts across the Great Plains. Arriving in California by year's end, he settled in San Francisco and began his career in journalism. Bierce soon gained notoriety as a sharp-tongued, darkly humorous editorialist and social commentator in a column called "The Town Crier," published regularly in the *San Francisco News-Letter and California Advertiser.* He rose to the editorship of the *News-Letter* and published his first short story, "The Haunted Valley," before leaving for England with his new wife, Mary Ellen "Mollie" Day, in 1871.

The Bierces spent the next three years in England, where he collected his writings into three volumes of essays, satires, and short stories—*The Fiend's Delight* (1873), *Nuggets and Dust Panned Out in California* (1873), and *Cobwebs from an Empty Skull* (1874). Returning to San Francisco in 1876, he continued to publish scathing commentaries and reviews, now in a column called "The Prattler" for *Argonaut* magazine. The following year, newspaper magnate William Randolph Hearst hired him to write for the *Examiner,* where he would remain for the next 20 years.

It was during this period that Bierce wrote most of the material for which he is best remembered. With virtually unchecked editorial freedom, he kept "The Prattler" as the name of his column and stepped up his caustic campaign against oppression and corruption in any domain: politics, government, the law, big business, and religion. He was thrust into the national spotlight on several occasions, usually for the controversial nature of his writings. In 1896, Hearst sent him to Washington, D.C., to expose the bribes and deceptions behind a bill being pushed by industrialist Collis P. Huntington that would have forgiven massive debts incurred by the builders of the Transcontinental Railroad; the bill was defeated. In 1898, Bierce became an outspoken opponent of the Spanish-American War even though Hearst had launched a major journalistic campaign to urge U.S. participation. Bierce remained a critic of U.S. military endeavors throughout the next decade.

Regarded by contemporaries as a writer's writer, Bierce cemented his reputation as both a cynic and a prose stylist with *The Devil's Dictionary* (1911), a collection of satirical definitions drawn from old newspaper columns that reflected his personal motto—"Nothing Matters"—and rank pessimism. Thus, by his definition, birth was "the first and direst of all disasters," and an optimist was "a proponent of the doctrine that black is white."

Restless at the age of 71, Bierce traveled to Mexico in December 1913 to witness the populist revolution being led by Pancho Villa. According to one rumor at the time, he died fighting alongside Villa; according to another theory, Villa himself shot Bierce following an argument over military strategy. Whatever the circumstances, Bierce was never seen or heard from again.

Robert Dobler and Fabio Lopez-Lazaro

See also: Realism

Definitions from *The Devil's Dictionary*, 1911

Once described as "the forgotten brother of Mark Twain" because of his irreverent satire and sheer skill as a writer, Ambrose Bierce is best known for The Devil's Dictionary *(1911), a compendium of more than 1,000 definitions of common words and phrases—from "abasement" to "zany"—in which he skewers politics, social convention, and everyday human folly. The first 500 definitions (A–L) were collected under the title* The Cynic's Word Book *in 1906. The expanded and retitled edition five years later proved much more successful. A selection of definitions follows.*

ACADEME, n. An ancient school where morality and philosophy were taught.

ACADEMY, n. [from ACADEME] A modern school where football is taught.

APOLOGIZE, v.i. To lay the foundation for a future offence.

BABE or BABY, n. A misshapen creature of no particular age, sex, or condition, chiefly remarkable for the violence of the sympathies and antipathies it excites in others, itself without sentiment or emotion.

BATTLE, n. A method of untying with the teeth of a political knot that would not yield to the tongue.

BORE, n. A person who talks when you wish him to listen.

BRAIN, n. An apparatus with which we think what we think. That which distinguishes the man who is content to *be* something from the man who wishes to *do* something. A man of great wealth, or one who has been pitchforked into high station, has commonly such a headful of brain that his neighbors cannot keep their hats on. In our civilization, and under our republican form of government, brain is so highly honored that it is rewarded by exemption from the cares of office.

CAPITAL, n. The seat of misgovernment. That which provides the fire, the pot, the dinner, the table and the knife and fork for the anarchist; the part of the repast that himself supplies is the disgrace before meat.

CHILDHOOD, n. The period of human life intermediate between the idiocy of infancy and the folly of youth—two removes from the sin of manhood and three from the remorse of age.

COMMERCE, n. A kind of transaction in which A plunders from B the goods of C, and for compensation B picks the pocket of D of money belonging to E.

CONSERVATIVE, n. A statesman who is enamored of existing evils, as distinguished from the Liberal, who wishes to replace them with others.

CORPORATION, n. An ingenious device for obtaining individual profit without individual responsibility.

DELUSION, n. The father of a most respectable family, comprising Enthusiasm, Affection, Self-denial, Faith, Hope, Charity and many other goodly sons and daughters.

DESTINY, n. A tyrant's authority for crime and fool's excuse for failure.

ECONOMY, n. Purchasing the barrel of whiskey that you do not need for the price of the cow that you cannot afford.

EDUCATION, n. That which discloses to the wise and disguises from the foolish their lack of understanding.

EMOTION, n. A prostrating disease caused by a determination of the heart to the head. It is sometimes accompanied by a copious discharge of hydrated chloride of sodium from the eyes.

FAMOUS, adj. Conspicuously miserable.

FUTURE, n. That period of time in which our affairs prosper, our friends are true and our happiness is assured.

GRAMMAR, n. A system of pitfalls thoughtfully prepared for the feet for the self-made man, along the path by which he advances to distinction.

HAPPINESS, n. An agreeable sensation arising from contemplating the misery of another.

HEAVEN, n. A place where the wicked cease from troubling you with talk of their personal affairs, and the good listen with attention while you expound your own.

HISTORY, n. An account mostly false, of events mostly unimportant, which are brought about by rulers mostly knaves, and soldiers mostly fools.

IDIOT, n. A member of a large and powerful tribe whose influence in human affairs has always been dominant and controlling. The Idiot's activity is not confined to any special field of thought or action, but "pervades and regulates the whole." He has the last word in everything; his decision is unappealable....

JUSTICE, n. A commodity which is a more or less adulterated condition the State sells to the citizen as a reward for his allegiance, taxes and personal service.

KISS, n. A word invented by the poets as a rhyme for "bliss." It is supposed to signify, in a general way, some kind of rite or ceremony appertaining to a good understanding; but the manner of its performance is unknown to this lexicographer.

LANGUAGE, n. The music with which we charm the serpents guarding another's treasure.

LAUGHTER, n. An interior convulsion, producing a distortion of the features and accompanied by inarticulate noises. It is infectious and, though intermittent, incurable. Liability to attacks of laughter is one of the characteristics distinguishing man from the animals....

LAWYER, n. One skilled in circumvention of the law.

LEARNING, n. The kind of ignorance distinguishing the studious.

LIFE, n. A spiritual pickle preserving the body from decay. We live in daily apprehension of its loss; yet when lost it is not missed. The question, "Is life worth living?" has been much discussed; particularly by those who think it is not, many of whom have written at great length in support of their view and by careful observance of the laws of health enjoyed for long terms of years the honors of successful controversy.

LOVE, n. A temporary insanity curable by marriage or by removal of the patient from the influences under which he incurred the disorder. This disease, like *caries* and many other ailments, is prevalent only among civilized races living under artificial conditions; barbarous nations breathing pure air and eating simple food enjoy immunity from its ravages. It is sometimes fatal, but more frequently to the physician than to the patient.

MAN, n. An animal so lost in rapturous contemplation of what he thinks he is as to overlook what he indubitably ought to be. His chief occupation is extermination of other animals and his own species, which, however, multiplies with such insistent rapidity as to infest the whole habitable earth and Canada.

MIRACLE, n. An act or event out of the order of nature and unaccountable, as beating a normal hand of four kings and an ace with four aces and a king.

MONEY, n. A blessing that is of no advantage to us excepting when we part with it. An evidence of culture and a passport to polite society.

NOSE, n. The extreme outpost of the face. From the circumstance that great conquerors have great noses, Getius, whose writings antedate the age of humor, calls the nose the organ of quell. It has been observed that one's nose is never so happy as when thrust into the affairs of others, from which some physiologists have drawn the inference that the nose is devoid of the sense of smell.

OPTIMISM, n. The doctrine, or belief, that everything is beautiful, including what is ugly, everything good, especially the bad, and everything right that is wrong. It is held with greatest tenacity by those most accustomed to the mischance of falling into adversity....

PEACE, n. In international affairs, a period of cheating between two periods of fighting.

PHILANTHROPIST, n. A rich (and usually bald) old gentleman who has trained himself to grin while his conscience is picking his pocket.

POLITICS, n. A strife of interests masquerading as a contest of principles. The conduct of public affairs for private advantage.

POLITICIAN, n. An eel in the fundamental mud upon which the superstructure of organized society is reared. When [he] wriggles he mistakes the agitation of his tail for the trembling of the edifice. As compared with the statesman, he suffers the disadvantage of being alive.

REALISM, n. The art of depicting nature as it is seen by toads. The charm suffusing a landscape painted by a mole, or a story written by a measuring-worm.

REASON, v. To weight probabilities in the scales of desire.

REPRESENTATIVE, n. In national politics, a member of the Lower House in this world, and without discernible hope of promotion in the next.

SENATE, n. A body of elderly gentlemen charged with high duties and misdemeanors.

TELEPHONE, n. An invention of the devil which abrogates some of the advantages of making a disagreeable person keep his distance.

TRUTH, n. An ingenious compound of desirability and appearance. Discovery of truth is the sole purpose of philosophy, which is the most ancient occupation of the human mind and has a fair prospect of existing with increasing activity to the end of time.

UN-AMERICAN, adj. Wicked, intolerable, heathenish.

VOTE, n. The instrument and symbol of a freeman's power to make a fool of himself and a wreck of his country.

WEATHER, n. The climate of the hour. A permanent topic of conversation among persons whom it does not interest, but who have inherited the tendency to chatter about it from naked arboreal ancestors whom it keenly concerned. The setting up official weather bureaus and their maintenance in mendacity prove that even governments are accessible to suasion by the rude forefathers of the jungle.

Sources: Project Gutenberg (www.gutenberg.org); Ambrose Bierce, *The Devil's Dictionary* (Cleveland: World Publishing Company, 1911).

Cather, Willa

(1873–1947)

Known for her depictions of pioneer life on the Great Plains and the deserts of the Southwest, novelist and short-story writer Willa Cather brought to life some of the neglected aspects of American settlement history, regional landscape, and European immigrant culture. In such novels as *O Pioneers!* (1913), *My Ántonia* (1918), and *Death Comes for the Archbishop* (1927), she combined a lustrous prose style and often irregular narrative structure in portraying the struggle of Old World immigrants to survive and assimilate on the arid American frontier.

Willa Sibert Cather was born in Back Creek Valley, near Winchester, Virginia, on December 7, 1873. The family moved to a ranch in south-central Nebraska when Cather was 9 years old and to the nearby town of Red Cloud the following year. Life on the Nebraska prairie would become the focus of much of her writing; the land itself would be a central feature and much beloved character in its own right, shaping the narrative.

Growing up among the immigrant farmers of the region, Cather was educated at home and in local public schools before entering the University of Nebraska–Lincoln in September 1890. She began with the goal of studying medicine but changed course after the *Nebraska State Journal* published one of her literary essays. It was at that moment, she later recalled, that she decided to become a writer. Supporting herself in college by writing for local newspapers, she graduated with a B.A. in English in 1895.

In 1896, at age 22, Cather left Nebraska for Pittsburgh, Pennsylvania, and a job as editor of the *Home Monthly* magazine. This was followed by work on the *Pittsburgh Daily Leader* and later in New York City as managing editor of the popular *McClure's Magazine*, the nation's foremost vehicle of muckraking journalism. All the while, Cather had been pursuing her interests in short fiction and poetry.

51

In a trilogy of acclaimed novels, Willa Cather evoked the landscape of the Great Plains where she was raised and the experience of European immigrants hewing a life there.

Her first book was a self-published volume of verse in 1903, *April Twilights,* followed two years later by a collection of short stories titled *The Troll Garden,* published by McClure.

Unfulfilled by the magazine business and passionate about fiction, Cather left journalism at age 37 upon the advice of New England novelist and friend Sarah Orne Jewett to pursue her writing full-time. *McClure's Magazine* serialized her first novel, *Alexander's Bridge* (1912), a moderately well-reviewed romance about a construction engineer facing a midlife crisis. After a two-month visit to Red Cloud that revived childhood memories, Cather produced what she called her "real" first novel, based on original material. *O Pioneers!,* a story of Swedish and German farmers hewing a life on the high plains at the turn of the twentieth century, earned favorable reviews and sustained Cather in her choice of career and creative direction. "I decided not to 'write' at all," she later said, "but simply to give myself up to the pleasure of recapturing in memory people and places I'd forgotten."

Living in an apartment in New York's Greenwich Village from 1912 to 1927, Cather produced a total of eight novels and one short-story collection. Following on the success of *O Pioneers!*, she completed her acclaimed Prairie Trilogy with *The Song of the Lark* (1915), another story set largely on the frontier (Colorado), about the development of an opera singer; and her masterwork, *My Ántonia,* revolving around a Bohemian immigrant girl loosely modeled on one of Cather's childhood friends. Told through the eyes of a male narrator, Jim Burden, whose love for the land parallels his love for Ántonia, the story captures Cather's own feelings when she left Nebraska.

Cather was awarded the 1923 Pulitzer Prize for Fiction for her next novel, *One of Ours* (1922), about the idealistic son of a Midwestern farmer who finds his calling on the battlefields of France during World War II. And in *Death Comes for the Archbishop,* the climax of her career as a novelist, Cather shifts her vision of the pioneering spirit to the Southwest and the efforts of two French clerics in establishing a Catholic diocese in the New Mexico Territory.

After three more novels, several more short-story collections, a volume of miscellaneous essays, and a host of awards, citations, and honorary degrees, Cather died at her home in New York City on April 24, 1947. Nearly seven decades later, in 2013, many details of the life and personality of an exceedingly private person were revealed in an anthology of previously unpublished correspondence, *The Selected Letters of Willa Cather.*

Jennifer Harrison and Jeff Hacker

Book I, Chapter Four, *My Ántonia*, 1918

A rich evocation of the pioneering spirit and the hardscrabble life of immigrant homesteaders on the Midwestern prairie, Willa Cather's novel My Ántonia *is, no less, an ode to the land itself. In Chapter Four of Book I, narrator Jim Burden recalls his youthful pony rides across the rolling fields to visit his Bohemian neighbors, the Shimerdas, and their daughter*

Ántonia—whose energy and enthusiasm epitomize the vitality of that place in that time. Otto Fuchs is the Burden family's hired hand; Krajiek is a Bohemian from whom the Shimerdas bought their farm; Dude is Jim's pony.

On the afternoon of that same Sunday I took my first long ride on my pony, under Otto's direction. After that Dude and I went twice a week to the post-office, six miles east of us, and I saved the men a good deal of time by riding on errands to our neighbours. When we had to borrow anything, or to send about word that there would be preaching at the sod schoolhouse, I was always the messenger. Formerly Fuchs attended to such things after working hours.

All the years that have passed have not dimmed my memory of that first glorious autumn. The new country lay open before me: there were no fences in those days, and I could choose my own way over the grass uplands, trusting the pony to get me home again. Sometimes I followed the sunflower-bordered roads. Fuchs told me that the sunflowers were introduced into that country by the Mormons; that at the time of the persecution, when they left Missouri and struck out into the wilderness to find a place where they could worship God in their own way, the members of the first exploring party, crossing the plains to Utah, scattered sunflower seed as they went. The next summer, when the long trains of wagons came through with all the women and children, they had the sunflower trail to follow. I believe that botanists do not confirm Fuchs's story, but insist that the sunflower was native to those plains. Nevertheless, that legend has stuck in my mind, and sunflower-bordered roads always seem to me the roads to freedom.

I used to love to drift along the pale-yellow cornfields, looking for the damp spots one sometimes found at their edges, where the smartweed soon turned a rich copper colour and the narrow brown leaves hung curled like cocoons about the swollen joints of the stem. Sometimes I went south to visit our German neighbours and to admire their catalpa grove, or to see the big elm tree that grew up out of a deep crack in the earth and had a hawk's nest in its branches. Trees were so rare in that country, and they had to make such a hard fight to grow, that we used to feel anxious about them, and visit them as if they were persons. It must have been the scarcity of detail in that tawny landscape that made detail so precious.

Sometimes I rode north to the big prairie-dog town to watch the brown earth-owls fly home in the late afternoon and go down to their nests underground with the dogs. Ántonia Shimerda liked to go with me, and we used to wonder a great deal about these birds of subterranean habit. We had to be on our guard there, for rattlesnakes were always lurking about. They came to pick up an easy living among the dogs and owls, which were quite defence-less against them; took possession of their comfortable houses and ate the eggs and puppies. We felt sorry for the owls. It was always mournful to see them come flying home at sunset and disappear under the earth. But, after all, we felt, winged things who would live like that must be rather degraded creatures. The dog-town was a long way from any pond or creek. Otto Fuchs said he had seen populous dog-towns in the desert where there was no surface water for fifty miles; he insisted that some of the holes must go down to water—nearly two hundred feet, here-abouts. Ántonia said she didn't believe it; that the dogs probably lapped up the dew in the early morning, like the rabbits.

Ántonia had opinions about everything, and she was soon able to make them known. Almost every day she came running across the prairie to have her reading lesson with me. Mrs. Shimerda grumbled, but realized it was important that one member of the family should learn English. When the lesson was over, we used to go up to the watermelon patch behind the garden. I split the melons with an old corn-knife, and we lifted out the hearts and ate them with the juice trickling through our fingers. The white Christmas melons we did not touch, but we watched them with curiosity. They were to be picked late, when the hard frosts had set in, and put away for winter use. After weeks on the ocean, the Shimerdas were famished for fruit. The two girls would wander for miles along the edge of the cornfields, hunting for ground-cherries.

Ántonia loved to help grandmother in the kitchen and to learn about cooking and housekeeping. She would stand beside her, watching her every movement. We were willing to believe that Mrs. Shimerda was a good housewife in her own country, but she managed poorly under new conditions: the conditions were bad enough, certainly!

I remember how horrified we were at the sour, ashy-grey bread she gave her family to eat. She mixed her dough, we discovered, in an old tin peck-measure that Krajiek had used about the barn. When she took the paste out to bake it, she left smears of dough sticking to the sides of the measure, put the measure on the shelf behind the stove, and let this residue ferment. The next time she made bread, she scraped this sour stuff down into the fresh dough to serve as yeast.

During those first months the Shimerdas never went to town. Krajiek encouraged them in the belief that in Black Hawk they would somehow be mysteriously separated from their money. They hated Krajiek, but they clung to him because he was the only human being with whom they could talk or from whom they could get information. He slept with the old man and the two boys in the dugout barn, along with the oxen. They kept him in their hole and fed him for the same reason that the prairie-dogs and the brown owls house the rattlesnakes—because they did not know how to get rid of him.

Sources: Project Gutenberg (www.gutenberg.org); Willa Cather, *My Ántonia* (Boston: Houghton Mifflin, 1918).

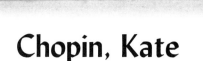

Chopin, Kate

(1851–1904)

An early feminist short-story writer and novelist, Kate Chopin drew often hostile reviews for her colorful depictions of Creole and Cajun life and did not gain recognition as a leading American author until years after her death. Even at that, the work with which she is most associated, the novel *The Awakening* (1899), was well ahead of its time in its views of female independence and sexual desire and remained out of print for decades. Discouraged by the critical and popular response, Chopin all but abandoned writing after its publication and died five years later. It was not until the 1960s that *The Awakening* and her short stories came to be fully appreciated for their local color, narrative power, and treatment of social themes—especially racism and female identity in Southern plantation culture.

She was born Katherine O'Flaherty in St. Louis on February 8, 1851, the third of five children. Her father was an Irish immigrant and successful businessman; her mother was of French Canadian and Creole extraction. She grew up speaking both English and French and felt comfortable in the two cultures. After her father's death in 1855, Kate attended the Academy of the Sacred Heart in St. Louis, where she came under the influence of the Catholic sisters until graduating in 1868. Her mother, grandmother, and classmate Kitty Garasché were other strong female presences as she grew up—especially during the Civil War years—and had an enduring influence on her life and writing. Kate also became a voracious reader.

At age 19, she met and married a young cotton trader and plantation manager named Otis Chopin, from Natchitoches Parish, Louisiana. Over the course of the next nine years, she gave birth to five sons and a daughter. The times were tough in Louisiana during Reconstruction, however, and her husband's cotton brokerage failed in 1879. The family moved to the town of Cloutierville in Natchitoches Parish, where he ran a general store and she raised the family—while soaking in the local color and way of life.

Otis Chopin died of malaria in 1882, leaving Kate as a widow with six children at age 32. She returned to St. Louis early the next year and took up writing to support the family. From the beginning, the Creole and Cajun experience of rural Louisiana formed the heart and soul of her fiction. Her stories for children appeared in such magazines as *Youth's Companion*, followed by pieces for adult readers in the *St. Louis Post Dispatch* and *Vogue*, *Harper's*, and *The Century* magazines. Chopin published a total of about 100 stories, essays, and sketches in a short career; more than 40 pieces of short fiction appeared in two collections, *Bayou Folk* (1894) and *A Night in Acadie* (1897). Both books gained minor notice for regional writing and earned Chopin a place in St. Louis's literary and cultural circles.

Like many of her short stories, Chopin's two novels—*At Fault* (published privately, 1890) and *The Awakening*—depict southern Louisiana life in spare, unsentimental prose with a heavy dose of local dialect, while conveying the inner experience of female protagonists in more subtle, complex terms. *At Fault* is about a Catholic widow in her thirties who falls in love with a married man. *The Awakening* is the story of a young woman dissatisfied in marriage who undergoes a sexual awakening, has an adulterous affair, and finally takes her own life.

The Awakening caused a scandal that shattered Chopin's reputation and effectively ended her writing career. Her publisher withdrew plans to publish a third short-fiction collection (which finally appeared in 1991), and she produced only a handful of stories in her remaining years. Chopin died on August 22, 1904, two days after suffering a cerebral hemorrhage at the Louisiana Purchase Exposition (St. Louis World's Fair).

Jeff Hacker

"Désirée's Baby," 1893

Kate Chopin's most widely read short story, first appearing in Vogue *magazine on January 14, 1893, "Désirée's Baby" is a tale of miscegenation in Creole Louisiana during the era before the Civil War. Aside from its depiction of a unique cultural setting and way of life, the story evokes the dark reality and destructive power of racism in the antebellum South. No less central to the narrative is the struggle for identity and self-worth on the part of its female protagonist—a recurring theme for a writer far ahead of her time.*

As the day was pleasant, Madame Valmondé drove over to L'Abri to see Désirée and the baby.

It made her laugh to think of Désirée with a baby. Why, it seemed but yesterday that Désirée was little more than a baby herself; when Monsieur in riding through the gateway of Valmondé had found her lying asleep in the shadow of the big stone pillar.

The little one awoke in his arms and began to cry for "Dada." That was as much as she could do or say. Some people thought she might have strayed there of her own accord, for she was of the toddling age. The prevailing belief was that she had been purposely left by a party of Texans, whose canvas-covered wagon, late in the day, had crossed the ferry that Coton Mais kept, just below the plantation. In time Madame Valmondé abandoned every speculation but the one that Désirée had been sent to her by a beneficent Providence to be the child of her affection, seeing that she was without child of the flesh. For the girl grew to be beautiful and gentle, affectionate and sincere,—the idol of Valmondé.

It was no wonder, when she stood one day against the stone pillar in whose shadow she had lain asleep, eighteen years before, that Armand Aubigny riding by and seeing her there, had fallen in love with her. That was the way all the Aubignys fell in love, as if struck by a pistol shot. The wonder was that he had not loved her before; for he had known her since his father brought him home from Paris, a boy of eight, after his mother died there. The passion that awoke in him that day, when he saw her at the gate, swept along like an avalanche, or like a prairie fire, or like anything that drives headlong over all obstacles.

Monsieur Valmondé grew practical and wanted things well considered: that is, the girl's obscure origin. Armand looked into her eyes and did not care. He was reminded that she was nameless. What did it matter about a name when he could give her one of the oldest and proudest in Louisiana? He ordered the corbeille from Paris, and contained himself with what patience he could until it arrived; then they were married.

Madame Valmondé had not seen Désirée and the baby for four weeks. When she reached L'Abri she shuddered at the first sight of it, as she always did. It was a sad looking place, which for many years had not known the gentle presence of a mistress, old Monsieur Aubigny having married and buried his wife in France, and she having loved her own land too well ever to leave it. The roof came down steep and black like a cowl, reaching out beyond the wide galleries that encircled the yellow stuccoed house. Big, solemn oaks grew close to it, and their thick-leaved, far-reaching branches shadowed it like a pall. Young Aubigny's rule was a strict one, too, and under it his negroes had forgotten how to be gay, as they had been during the old master's easy-going and indulgent lifetime.

The young mother was recovering slowly, and lay full length, in her soft white muslins and laces, upon a couch. The baby was beside her, upon her arm, where he had fallen asleep, at her breast. The yellow nurse woman sat beside a window fanning herself.

Madame Valmondé bent her portly figure over Désirée and kissed her, holding her an instant tenderly in her arms. Then she turned to the child.

"This is not the baby!" she exclaimed, in startled tones. French was the language spoken at Valmondé in those days.

"I knew you would be astonished," laughed Désirée, "at the way he has grown. The little cochon de lait! Look at his legs, mamma, and his hands and fingernails,—real finger-nails. Zandrine had to cut them this morning. Isn't it true, Zandrine?"

The woman bowed her turbaned head majestically, "Mais si, Madame."

"And the way he cries," went on Désirée, "is deafening. Armand heard him the other day as far away as La Blanche's cabin."

Madame Valmondé had never removed her eyes from the child. She lifted it and walked with it over to the window that was lightest. She scanned the baby narrowly, then looked as searchingly at Zandrine, whose face was turned to gaze across the fields.

When the baby was about three months old, Désirée awoke one day to the conviction that there was something in the air menacing her peace.

"Yes, the child has grown, has changed," said Madame Valmondé, slowly, as she replaced it beside its mother. "What does Armand say?"

Désirée's face became suffused with a glow that was happiness itself.

"Oh, Armand is the proudest father in the parish, I believe, chiefly because it is a boy, to bear his name; though he says not,—that he would have loved a girl as well. But I know it isn't true. I know he says that to please me. And mamma," she added, drawing Madame Valmondé's head down to her, and speaking in a whisper, "he hasn't punished one of them—not one of them—since baby is born. Even Negrillon, who pretended to have burnt his leg that he might rest from work—he only laughed, and said Negrillon was a great scamp. Oh, mamma, I'm so happy; it frightens me."

What Désirée said was true. Marriage, and later the birth of his son had softened Armand Aubigny's imperious and exacting nature greatly. This was what made the gentle Désirée so happy, for she loved him desperately. When he frowned she trembled, but loved him. When he smiled, she asked no greater blessing of God. But Armand's dark, handsome face had not often been disfigured by frowns since the day he fell in love with her.

When the baby was about three months old, Désirée awoke one day to the conviction that there was something in the air menacing her peace. It was at first too subtle to grasp. It had only been a disquieting suggestion; an air of mystery among the blacks; unexpected visits from far-off neighbors who could hardly account for their coming. Then a strange, an awful change in her husband's manner, which she dared not ask him to explain. When he spoke to her, it was with averted eyes, from which the old love-light seemed to have gone out. He absented himself from home; and when there, avoided her presence and that of her child, without excuse. And the very spirit of Satan seemed suddenly to take hold of him in his dealings with the slaves. Désirée was miserable enough to die.

She sat in her room, one hot afternoon, in her peignoir, listlessly drawing through her fingers the strands of her long, silky brown hair that hung about her shoulders. The baby, half naked, lay asleep upon her own great mahogany bed, that was like a sumptuous throne, with its satin-lined half-canopy. One of La Blanche's little quadroon boys—half naked too—stood fanning the child slowly with a fan of peacock feathers. Désirée's eyes had been fixed absently and sadly upon the baby, while she was striving to penetrate the threatening mist that she felt closing about her. She looked from her child to the boy who stood beside him, and back again; over and over. "Ah!" It was a cry that she could not help; which she was not conscious of having uttered. The blood turned like ice in her veins, and a clammy moisture gathered upon her face.

She tried to speak to the little quadroon boy; but no sound would come, at first. When he heard his name uttered, he looked up, and his mistress was pointing to the door. He laid aside the great, soft fan, and obediently stole away, over the polished floor, on his bare tiptoes.

She stayed motionless, with gaze riveted upon her child, and her face the picture of fright.

Presently her husband entered the room, and without noticing her, went to a table and began to search among some papers which covered it.

"Armand," she called to him, in a voice which must have stabbed him, if he was human. But he did not notice. "Armand," she said again. Then she rose and tottered towards him.

"Armand," she panted once more, clutching his arm, "look at our child. What does it mean? tell me."

He coldly but gently loosened her fingers from about his arm and thrust the hand away from him. "Tell me what it means!" she cried despairingly.

"It means," he answered lightly, "that the child is not white; it means that you are not white."

A quick conception of all that this accusation meant for her nerved her with unwonted courage to deny it. "It is a lie; it is not true, I am white! Look at my hair, it is brown; and my eyes are gray, Armand, you know they are gray. And my skin is fair," seizing his wrist. "Look at my hand; whiter than yours, Armand," she laughed hysterically.

"As white as La Blanche's," he returned cruelly; and went away leaving her alone with their child.

When she could hold a pen in her hand, she sent a despairing letter to Madame Valmondé.

"My mother, they tell me I am not white. Armand has told me I am not white. For God's sake tell them it is not true. You must know it is not true. I shall die. I must die. I cannot be so unhappy, and live."

The answer that came was brief:

"My own Désirée: Come home to Valmondé; back to your mother who loves you. Come with your child."

When the letter reached Désirée she went with it to her husband's study, and laid it open upon the desk before which he sat. She was like a stone image: silent, white, motionless after she placed it there.

In silence he ran his cold eyes over the written words.

He said nothing. "Shall I go, Armand?" she asked in tones sharp with agonized suspense.

"Yes, go."

"Do you want me to go?"

"Yes, I want you to go."

He thought Almighty God had dealt cruelly and unjustly with him; and felt, somehow, that he was paying Him back in kind when he stabbed thus into his wife's soul. Moreover he no longer loved her, because of the unconscious injury she had brought upon his home and his name.

She turned away like one stunned by a blow, and walked slowly towards the door, hoping he would call her back.

"Good-by, Armand," she moaned.

He did not answer her. That was his last blow at fate.

Désirée went in search of her child. Zandrine was pacing the sombre gallery with it. She took the little one from the nurse's arms with no word of explanation, and descending the steps, walked away, under the live-oak branches.

It was an October afternoon; the sun was just sinking. Out in the still fields the negroes were picking cotton.

Désirée had not changed the thin white garment nor the slippers which she wore. Her hair was uncovered and the sun's rays brought a golden gleam from its brown meshes. She did not take the broad, beaten road which led to the far-off plantation of Valmondé. She walked across a deserted field, where the stubble bruised her tender feet, so delicately shod, and tore her thin gown to shreds.

She disappeared among the reeds and willows that grew thick along the banks of the deep, sluggish bayou; and she did not come back again.

Some weeks later there was a curious scene enacted at L'Abri. In the centre of the smoothly swept back yard was a great bonfire. Armand Aubigny sat in the wide hallway that commanded a view of the spectacle; and it was he who dealt out to a half dozen negroes the material which kept this fire ablaze.

A graceful cradle of willow, with all its dainty furbishings, was laid upon the pyre, which had already been fed with the richness of a priceless layette. Then there were silk gowns, and velvet and satin ones added to these; laces, too, and embroideries; bonnets and gloves; for the corbeille had been of rare quality.

The last thing to go was a tiny bundle of letters; innocent little scribblings that Désirée had sent to him during the days of their espousal. There was the remnant of one back in the drawer from which he took them. But it was not Désirée's; it was part of an old letter from his mother to his father. He read it. She was thanking God for the blessing of her husband's love: a—

"But above all," she wrote, "night and day, I thank the good God for having so arranged our lives that our dear Armand will never know that his mother, who adores him, belongs to the race that is cursed with the brand of slavery."

Sources: Kate Chopin International Society (www.katechopin.org); Electronic Text Center, University of Virginia Library (http://etext.lib.virginia.edu).

Crane, Stephen
(1871–1900)

Novelist, short-story writer, journalist, and poet Stephen Crane is known as a literary innovator whose first two novels—*Maggie: A Girl of the Streets* (1893) and *The Red Badge of Courage* (1895)—mark the rise of naturalism as a major movement in American fiction. Although he died at the age of 28, Crane produced several works of lasting influence. His writing broke ground for the kind of sociological urban novels produced by Theodore Dreiser and Frank Norris and later came to be recognized for its influence on the modernist movement.

Born in Newark, New Jersey, on November 1, 1871, Crane was the fourteenth and youngest child of a Methodist minister and his devout Methodist wife. Crane's father died when he was 8 years old, leaving his mother to raise the entire family. Frail and introspective, "Stevie" Crane began writing at an early age and, by 16, had published articles in the *New York Tribune* on street life in the city. He gained further writing experience while working for his older brother Townley, who owned a reporting agency in Asbury Park, New Jersey.

After briefly attending Lafayette College and Syracuse University, Crane left school upon the death of his mother in 1890 and took up a bohemian existence as a freelance writer in New York City. His first novel, *Maggie: A Girl of the Streets,* was an unflinching portrait of a slum prostitute and a grim look at Irish immigrant life in the Bowery section of lower Manhattan. With money inherited from his mother, Crane self-published the first 1,100 copies of the novel under the pen name Johnston Smith. *Maggie* sold poorly but received a stunning review by the respected critic William Dean Howells, who called it "a wonderful book" and compared Crane to the great Russian novelist Leo Tolstoy in his ability to understand and portray ordinary people and everyday lives.

In only a handful of works published over a single decade (1893–1903), Stephen Crane broke new ground in American fiction as a pioneer of naturalism and the true-to-life urban novel.

Crane's primary aim as a novelist was to express the "truth of life" through fiction. Thus, during the course of writing *Maggie*, he lived with tramps in immigrant neighborhoods, slept in a Bowery flophouse, and waited in a breadline with unemployed workers during a blizzard. In the starkly fatalistic spirit of naturalist fiction, he portrayed members of the lower working class as complete human beings victimized by their circumstances and capable of acts ranging from brutality and indifference to self-sacrifice and kindness.

Although Howells's praise lifted Crane's spirits at a time when he contemplated another means of livelihood, the young writer finally won widespread critical and commercial success by shifting his attention from the urban slums to the battlefields of the Civil War. A masterpiece of realistic imagination—Crane had never experienced the violence of the battlefield—*The Red Badge of Courage* recounts the inner struggle against a foot soldier's fear through the eyes of Union Private Henry Fleming. The triumph of *Red Badge*, which earned strong reviews for its realistic depiction of war, psychological authenticity, and original prose style, embroidered Crane permanently into the fabric of American literary history.

On the strength of *Red Badge* and a successful book of poems also published in 1895, *The Black Riders and Other Lines*, Crane began receiving high-profile newspaper assignments. Among these were stints as a correspondent in the Greco-Turkish War of 1897 and the Spanish-American War of 1898, accounts of which he collected in *Active Service* (1899) and *Wounds in the Rain: War Stories* (1900). The latter, together with the *Whilomville Stories* (1900), was published posthumously.

In the meantime, Crane continued writing fiction. An incident in 1896, in which the steamboat SS *Commodore* shipwrecked en route from Florida to Cuba and left Crane stranded in a dinghy with three other men for 30 hours, provided the raw material for his famous short story "The Open Boat" (1897). That work, which the English contemporary H.G. Wells called "the crown" of Crane's career, epitomized his view of human beings as helpless creatures who are subject to an inconstant, unknowable fate in an indifferent and often hostile universe. A similarly bleak view of the human condition permeates such other Crane short stories as "The Bride Comes to Yellow Sky" (1898), "The Blue Hotel" (1899), and "The Monster" (1899).

In 1898, still suffering from tuberculosis after his ordeal in the waters off Cuba, Crane moved to Sussex, England, with his mistress, the former proprietor of a brothel; the couple was married later that year. Crane was a celebrity in England, where he befriended such other literary lions as Wells, Joseph Conrad, and Henry James. Hastened by dissolute living, death came while he was seeking a cure for tuberculosis at a spa in Badenweiler, Germany, on June 5, 1900.

Bob Batchelor

See also: Dreiser, Theodore; Howells, William Dean; Naturalism

◇◇◇
Chapter Five, *Maggie: A Girl of the Streets*, 1893
◇◇◇

Stephen Crane's novel Maggie: A Girl of the Streets *set a trend for naturalist fiction with its portrayal of a lead character—a young girl in the Irish slums of New York City who is driven to prostitution—for whom there is no escape from social conditions and heredity. The grim fate of Maggie and other protagonists in naturalist novels thus constitutes a reversal of the American Dream as represented in the novels of Horatio Alger, for example, and the real-life aspirations of the millions of immigrants then arriving on U.S. shores. Maggie becomes the focus of Crane's novel in Chapter Five, emerging as a young beauty who attracts the attention of neighborhood boys and goes to work in a sweatshop. Her budding relationship with the boy Pete sparks her dream of life in a better place. The street vernacular employed throughout* Maggie *is one of the hallmarks of realist and naturalist American literature in the late nineteenth century.*

The girl, Maggie, blossomed in a mud puddle. She grew to be a most rare and wonderful production of a tenement district, a pretty girl.

None of the dirt of Rum Alley seemed to be in her veins. The philosophers up-stairs, down-stairs and on the same floor, puzzled over it.

When a child, playing and fighting with gamins in the street, dirt disguised her. Attired in tatters and grime, she went unseen.

There came a time, however, when the young men of the vicinity said: "Dat Johnson goil is a puty good looker." About this period her brother remarked to her: "Mag, I'll tell yeh dis! See? Yeh've edder got teh go teh hell or go teh work!" Whereupon she went to work, having the feminine aversion of going to hell.

By a chance, she got a position in an establishment where they made collars and cuffs. She received a stool and a machine in a room where sat twenty girls of various shades of yellow discontent. She perched on the stool and treadled at her machine all day, turning out collars, the name of whose brand could be noted for its irrelevancy to anything in connection with collars. At night she returned home to her mother.

Jimmie grew large enough to take the vague position of head of the family. As incumbent of that office, he stumbled up-stairs late at night, as his father had done before him. He reeled about the room, swearing at his relations, or went to sleep on the floor.

The mother had gradually arisen to that degree of fame that she could bandy words with her acquaintances among the police-justices. Court-officials called her by her first name. When she appeared they pursued a course which had been theirs for months. They invariably grinned and cried out: "Hello, Mary, you here again?" Her grey head wagged in many a court. She always besieged the bench with voluble excuses, explanations, apologies and prayers. Her flaming face and rolling eyes were a sort of familiar sight on the island. She measured time by means of sprees, and was eternally swollen and dishevelled.

One day the young man, Pete, who as a lad had smitten the Devil's Row urchin in the back of the head and put to flight the antagonists of his friend, Jimmie, strutted upon the scene. He met Jimmie one day on the street, promised to take him to a boxing match in Williamsburg, and called for him in the evening.

Maggie observed Pete.

He sat on a table in the Johnson home and dangled his checked legs with an enticing nonchalance. His hair was curled down over his forehead in an oiled bang. His rather pugged nose seemed to revolt from contact with a bristling moustache of short, wire-like hairs. His blue double-breasted coat, edged with black braid, buttoned close to a red puff tie, and his patent-leather shoes looked like murder-fitted weapons.

His mannerisms stamped him as a man who had a correct sense of his personal superiority. There was valor and contempt for circumstances in the glance of his eye. He waved his hands like a man of the world, who dismisses religion and philosophy, and says "Fudge." He had certainly seen everything and with each curl of his lip, he declared that it amounted to nothing. Maggie thought he must be a very elegant and graceful bartender.

He was telling tales to Jimmie.

Maggie watched him furtively, with half-closed eyes, lit with a vague interest.

"Hully gee! Dey makes me tired," he said. "Mos' e'ry day some farmer comes in an' tries teh run deh shop. See? But dey gits t'rowed right out! I jolt dem right out in deh street before dey knows where dey is! See?"

"Sure," said Jimmie.

"Dere was a mug come in deh place deh odder day wid an idear he wus goin' teh own deh place! Hully gee, he wus goin' teh own deh place! I see he had a still on an' I didn' wanna giv 'im no stuff, so I says: 'Git deh hell outa here an' don' make no trouble,' I says like dat! See? 'Git deh hell outa here an' don' make no trouble'; like dat. 'Git deh hell outa here,' I says. See?"

Jimmie nodded understandingly. Over his features played an eager desire to state the amount of his valor in a similar crisis, but the narrator proceeded.

"Well, deh blokie he says: 'T'hell wid it! I ain' lookin' for no scrap,' he says (See?), 'but' he says, 'I'm 'spectable cit'zen an' I wanna drink an' purtydamnsoon, too.' See? 'Deh hell,' I says. Like dat! 'Deh hell,' I says. See? 'Don' make no trouble,' I says. Like dat. 'Don' make no trouble.' See? Den deh mug he squared off an' said he was fine as silk wid his dukes (See?) an' he wanned a drink damnquick. Dat's what he said. See?"

"Sure," repeated Jimmie.

Pete continued. "Say, I jes' jumped deh bar an' deh way I plunked dat blokie was great. See? Dat's right! In deh jaw! See? Hully gee, he t'rowed a spittoon true deh front windee. Say, I taut I'd drop dead. But deh boss, he comes in after an' he says, 'Pete, yehs done jes' right! Yeh've gota keep order an' it's all right.' See? 'It's all right,' he says. Dat's what he said."

The two held a technical discussion.

"Dat bloke was a dandy," said Pete, in conclusion, "but he hadn' oughta made no trouble. Dat's what I says teh dem: 'Don' come in here an' make no trouble,' I says, like dat. 'Don' make no trouble.' See?"

As Jimmie and his friend exchanged tales descriptive of their prowess, Maggie leaned back in the shadow. Her eyes dwelt wonderingly and rather wistfully upon Pete's face. The broken furniture, grimey walls, and general disorder and dirt of her home of a sudden appeared before her and began to take a potential aspect. Pete's aristocratic person looked as if it might soil. She looked keenly at him, occasionally, wondering if he was feeling contempt. But Pete seemed to be enveloped in reminiscence.

"Hully gee," said he, "dose mugs can't phase me. Dey knows I kin wipe up deh street wid any t'ree of dem."

When he said, "Ah, what deh hell," his voice was burdened with disdain for the inevitable and contempt for anything that fate might compel him to endure.

Maggie perceived that here was the beau ideal of a man. Her dim thoughts were often searching for far away lands where, as God says, the little hills sing together in the morning. Under the trees of her dream-gardens there had always walked a lover.

Sources: Internet Archive (http://archive.org); Stephen Crane, *Maggie: A Girl of the Streets* (New York: D. Appleton and Company, 1896).

Dreiser, Theodore

(1871–1945)

A pioneer and leading practitioner of naturalist fiction, Theodore Dreiser captured the underside of modern urban-industrial life in starkly realistic terms. His bottom-up look at society in such novels as *Sister Carrie* (1900) and *An American Tragedy* (1925) shocked middle- and upper-class readers and revealed a parallel social universe operating beneath their immediate view. Like the works of such other naturalist writers as Stephen Crane, Upton Sinclair, Frank Norris, and Jack London, Dreiser's novels are characterized by journalistic attention to detail; characters driven by baser instincts; themes of crime, vice, and social conflict; and fatalistic story lines that show how larger forces overwhelm individual human will in modern American society.

The twelfth of 13 children, Herman Theodore Dreiser was born in Terre Haute, Indiana, on August 27, 1871. His father, John Paul Dreiser, was a stern German Catholic who had come to America to make his fortune but lost everything when his wool factory burned down in 1869. Dreiser's mother, Sarah Schanab, was a Mennonite from Ohio who had met and married John Paul when she was only 16. The future writer was raised Catholic and grew up in relative poverty; the family moved to several Indiana towns and Chicago in search of economic stability. At age 15, Dreiser dropped out of high school in Warsaw, Indiana, boarded a train, and moved to Chicago, where he worked a succession of odd jobs.

After a year at Indiana University in Bloomington (1889–1890), he returned to Chicago and in June 1892 landed work as a reporter for a local newspaper, the *Globe.* Although he never had a regular column, Dreiser's years as a big-city journalist—including stints at the *St. Louis Globe-Democrat,* the *St. Louis Republic,* and the *Pittsburgh Dispatch*—provided the gritty settings and stark themes of his later fiction and helped forge his hard-hitting prose style. Most of all, he

The novels of Theodore Dreiser marked a pinnacle in literary naturalism with their grim depictions of industrialized urban life and fatalistic stories of the defeat of individual will.

witnessed firsthand the brutalities that befell the lowest ranks of the urban working poor.

Leaving regular newspaper and magazine work in 1897, Dreiser began his career as a freelance writer, contributing articles to national magazines on a wide range of subjects—from modern art to the Chicago meatpacking business. Interviewing celebrities was one of his specialties; subjects included inventor Thomas Edison, literary critic and novelist William Dean Howells, and industrialists Andrew Carnegie and Philip Armour. In his off-hours, Dreiser was also trying his hand at poetry and short stories and began writing a novel. An editor who knew him at the time described him as "a writing machine." In the meantime, he had made New York City his permanent residence and in December 1898 married Missouri schoolteacher Sara White.

Dreiser's first novel, *Sister Carrie,* was a stunningly frank depiction of life in Chicago and a sympathetic, nonmoralizing portrayal of a naïve country girl whose pursuit of fame and fortune as an actress leads her into illicit affairs with two men. For Dreiser himself, the tragedy of *Sister Carrie* was the treatment of the manuscript by publisher Frank Doubleday, who deemed it too sordid for public consumption. Unwilling to alter the text, Dreiser insisted that Doubleday honor his contract and threatened a lawsuit. In response, Doubleday cut a number of passages from the book and printed 1,000 copies but did no advertising or promotion. The first edition sold fewer than 500 copies; the complete, uncensored version was not published until 1982.

The initial failure of *Sister Carrie,* combined with marital problems and the death of his parents, drove Dreiser to a nervous breakdown. His depression and inability to write lasted three years. With the help of his brother Paul, a successful songwriter and music composer, Dreiser recovered his spirits and resumed his career. By 1910, he was editing three women's magazines, had won critical acclaim for a re-release of *Sister Carrie,* and had completed his second novel, *Jennie Gerhardt* (1911). The new work, about a young woman who bears the illegitimate child of a U.S. senator, faced criticism and editing similar to that of *Sister Carrie* for its sexual candor, condemnation of society, and refusal to blame a "fallen woman."

In the years that followed, Dreiser resumed writing with his old fervor, publishing five works of fiction, four nonfiction books, and two plays between 1912 and 1925. With his third novel, *The Financier* (1912), he turned his focus more specifically to American social and economic institutions. *The Financier* was the first in his Cowperhood Trilogy (or Trilogy of Desire)—followed by *The Titan* (1914) and *The Stoic* (1947)—based on the life of Chicago financier and mass-transit tycoon Charles Tyson Yerkes. *The "Genius"* (1915), a semi-autobiographical novel, became the subject of a protracted legal battle after being censored for sexual content by the New York Society for the Suppression of Vice. Dreiser achieved his greatest critical and commercial success in 1925 with *An American Tragedy,* based on a notorious murder case in upstate New York. The story of an ambitious young man whose desire for wealth and status overwhelms his moral sense and compels him to murder his pregnant girlfriend, *An American Tragedy* once again conveyed Dreiser's view that materialistic society was as responsible for the wrongdoing as the protagonist himself.

Meanwhile, in the burgeoning artistic community of New York's Greenwich Village, Dreiser developed close relations with liberal thinkers and the artistic avant-garde of the 1910s and 1920s. He associated with socialists Max Eastman and Daniel DeLeon, supported the birth-control movement of Margaret Sanger, befriended anarchist Emma Goldman, and wrote for the radical political journal *The Masses* and the modernist aesthetic review *The Seven Arts*. He championed the cause of literary freedom, wrote extensively about his later travels to the Soviet Union, and continued his activism on a number of progressive fronts after moving to California in 1938. Dreiser died in Hollywood on December 28, 1945.

Bob Batchelor and Michael A. Rembis

See also: Crane, Stephen; London, Jack; Naturalism; Sinclair, Upton

◇◇

Chapter Three, "We Question of Fortune: Four-Fifty a Week," *Sister Carrie* (excerpt), 1900

◇◇

Considered the first great urban novel in America and one of the highest achievements of literary naturalism, Theodore Dreiser's Sister Carrie *shocked turn-of-the-century readers with its grimly realistic depiction of modern city life and the tragic effects of industrial society on the lives of the poor and working class. Especially offensive to some readers was the aspect of Dreiser's novel that defined it as a naturalist rather merely realist text: the implication that the characters are creatures of their social and economic environment, shaped by class, convention, and commercial forces, rather than directly accountable for their own moral failings. In Chapter Three, Dreiser describes the allure of city life for Carrie Meeber compared with the slow pace of the farm on which she grew up. The scene is a turning point for her, as she realizes in looking for a job "how much the city held—wealth, fashion, ease" and begins to feel "the drag of desire" for respectability, fortune, and fame. "His aim is not merely to tell a tale," wrote journalist and critic H.L. Mencken about Dreiser's first novel; "his aim is to show the vast ebb and flow of forces which sway and condition human destiny."*

Once across the river and into the wholesale district, she glanced about her for some likely door at which to apply. As she contemplated the wide windows and imposing signs, she became conscious of being gazed upon and understood for what she was—a wage-seeker. She had never done this thing before, and lacked courage. To avoid a certain indefinable shame she felt at being caught spying about for a position, she quickened her steps and assumed an air of indifference supposedly common to one upon an errand. In this way she passed many manufacturing and wholesale houses without once glancing in. At last, after several blocks of walking, she felt that this would not do, and began to look about again, though without relaxing her pace. A little way on she saw a great door which, for some reason, attracted her attention. It was ornamented by a small brass sign, and seemed to be the entrance to a vast hive of six or seven floors. "Perhaps," she thought, "they may want some one," and crossed over to enter. When she came within a score of feet of the desired goal, she saw through the window a young man in a grey checked suit. That he had anything to do with the concern, she could not tell, but because he happened to be looking in her direction her weakening heart misgave her and she hurried by, too overcome with shame to enter. Over the way stood a great six-story structure, labelled Storm and King, which she viewed with rising hope. It was a wholesale dry goods concern and employed women. She could see them moving about now and then upon the upper floors. This place she decided to enter, no matter what. She crossed over and walked directly toward the entrance. As she did so, two men came out and paused in the door. A telegraph messenger in blue dashed past her and up the few steps that led to the entrance and disappeared. Several pedestrians out of the hurrying throng which filled the sidewalks passed about her as she paused, hesitating. She looked helplessly around, and then, seeing herself observed, retreated. It was too difficult a task. She could not go past them.

So severe a defeat told sadly upon her nerves. Her feet carried her mechanically forward, every foot of her progress being a satisfactory portion of a flight which she gladly made. Block after block passed by. Upon street-lamps at the various corners she read names such as Madison, Monroe, La Salle, Clark, Dearborn, State, and still she went, her feet beginning to tire upon the broad stone flagging. She was pleased in part that the streets were bright and clean. The morning sun, shining down with steadily increasing warmth, made the shady side of the streets pleasantly cool. She looked at the blue sky overhead with more realisation of its charm than had ever come to her before.

Her cowardice began to trouble her in a way. She turned back, resolving to hunt up Storm and King and enter. On the way she encountered a great wholesale shoe company, through the broad plate windows of which she saw an enclosed executive department, hidden by frosted glass. Without this enclosure, but just within the street entrance, sat a grey-haired gentleman at a small table, with a large open ledger before him. She walked by this institution several times hesitating, but, finding herself unobserved, faltered past the screen door and stood humbly waiting.

"Well, young lady," observed the old gentleman, looking at her somewhat kindly, "what is it you wish?"

"I am, that is, do you—I mean, do you need any help?" she stammered.

"Not just at present," he answered smiling. "Not just at present. Come in some time next week. Occasionally we need some one."

She received the answer in silence and backed awkwardly out. The pleasant nature of her reception rather astonished her. She had expected that it would be more difficult, that something cold and harsh would be said—she knew not what. That she had not been put to shame and made to feel her unfortunate position, seemed remarkable.

Somewhat encouraged, she ventured into another large structure. It was a clothing company, and more people were in evidence—well-dressed men of forty and more, surrounded by brass railings.

An office boy approached her.

"Who is it you wish to see?" he asked.

"I want to see the manager," she said.

He ran away and spoke to one of a group of three men who were conferring together. One of these came towards her.

"Well?" he said coldly. The greeting drove all courage from her at once.

"Do you need any help?" she stammered.

"No," he replied abruptly, and turned upon his heel.

She went foolishly out, the office boy deferentially swinging the door for her, and gladly sank into the obscuring crowd. It was a severe setback to her recently pleased mental state.

Now she walked quite aimlessly for a time, turning here and there, seeing one great company after another, but finding no courage to prosecute her single inquiry. High noon came, and with it hunger. She hunted out an unassuming restaurant and entered, but was disturbed to find that the prices were exorbitant for the size of her purse. A bowl of soup was all that she could afford, and, with this quickly eaten, she went out again. It restored her strength somewhat and made her moderately bold to pursue the search.

In walking a few blocks to fix upon some probable place, she again encountered the firm of Storm and King, and this time managed to get in. Some gentlemen were conferring close at hand, but took no notice of her. She was left standing, gazing nervously upon the floor. When the limit of her distress had been nearly reached, she was beckoned to by a man at one of the many desks within the near-by railing.

"Who is it you wish to see?" he inquired.

"Why, any one, if you please," she answered. "I am looking for something to do."

"Oh, you want to see Mr. McManus," he returned. "Sit down," and he pointed to a chair against the neighbouring wall. He went on leisurely writing, until after a time a short, stout gentleman came in from the street.

"Mr. McManus," called the man at the desk, "this young woman wants to see you."

The short gentleman turned about towards Carrie, and she arose and came forward.

"What can I do for you, miss?" he inquired, surveying her curiously.

"I want to know if I can get a position," she inquired.

"As what?" he asked.

"Not as anything in particular," she faltered.

"Have you ever had any experience in the wholesale dry goods business?" he questioned.

"No, sir," she replied.

"Are you a stenographer or typewriter?"

"No, sir."

"Well, we haven't anything here," he said. "We employ only experienced help."

She began to step backward toward the door, when something about her plaintive face attracted him.

"Have you ever worked at anything before?" he inquired.

"No, sir," she said.

Each separate counter was a show place of dazzling interest and attraction. She could not help feeling the claim of each trinket and valuable. . . .

"Well, now, it's hardly possible that you would get anything to do in a wholesale house of this kind. Have you tried the department stores?"

She acknowledged that she had not.

"Well, if I were you," he said, looking at her rather genially, "I would try the department stores. They often need young women as clerks."

"Thank you," she said, her whole nature relieved by this spark of friendly interest.

"Yes," he said, as she moved toward the door, "you try the department stores," and off he went.

At that time the department store was in its earliest form of successful operation, and there were not many. The first three in the United States, established about 1884, were in Chicago. Carrie was familiar with the names of several through the advertisements in the "Daily News," and now proceeded to seek them. The words of Mr. McManus had somehow managed to restore her courage, which had fallen low, and she dared to hope that this new line would offer her something. Some time she spent in wandering up and down, thinking to encounter the buildings by chance, so readily is the mind, bent upon prosecuting a hard but needful errand, eased by that self-deception which the semblance of search, without the reality, gives. At last she inquired of a police officer, and was directed to proceed "two blocks up," where she would find "The Fair."

The nature of these vast retail combinations, should they ever permanently disappear, will form an interesting chapter in the commercial history of our nation. Such a flowering out of a modest trade principle the world had never witnessed up to that time. They were along the line of the most effective retail organisation, with hundreds of stores coordinated into one and laid out upon the most imposing and economic basis. They were handsome, bustling, successful affairs, with a host of clerks and a swarm of patrons. Carrie passed along the busy aisles, much affected by the remarkable displays of trinkets, dress goods, stationery, and jewelry. Each separate counter was a show place of dazzling interest and attraction. She could not help feeling the claim of each trinket and valuable upon her personally, and yet she did not stop. There was nothing there which she could not have used—nothing which she did not long to own. The dainty slippers and stockings, the delicately frilled skirts and petticoats, the laces, ribbons, hair-combs, purses, all touched her with individual desire, and she felt keenly the fact that not any of these things were in the range of her purchase. She was a work-seeker, an outcast without employment, one whom the average employee could tell at a glance was poor and in need of a situation.

It must not be thought that any one could have mistaken her for a nervous, sensitive, high-strung nature, cast unduly upon a cold, calculating, and unpoetic world. Such certainly she was not. But women are peculiarly sensitive to their adornment.

Not only did Carrie feel the drag of desire for all which was new and pleasing in apparel for women, but she noticed too, with a touch at the heart, the fine ladies who elbowed and ignored her, brushing past in utter disregard of her presence, themselves eagerly enlisted in the materials which the store contained. Carrie was not familiar with the appearance of her more fortunate sisters of the city. Neither had she before known the nature and appearance of the shop girls with whom she now compared poorly. They were pretty in the main, some even handsome, with an air of independence and indifference which added, in the case of the more favoured, a certain piquancy. Their clothes were neat, in many instances fine, and wherever she encountered the eye of one it was only to recognise in it a keen analysis of her own position—her individual shortcomings of dress and that shadow of *manner* which she thought must hang about her and make clear to all who and what she was. A flame of envy lighted in her heart. She realised in a dim way how much the city held—wealth, fashion, ease—every adornment for women, and she longed for dress and beauty with a whole heart.

Sources: Electronic Text Center, University of Virginia Library (http://etext.lib. virginia.edu); Theodore Dreiser, *Sister Carrie* (New York: Doubleday, Page & Co., 1900).

Du Bois, W.E.B.

(1868–1963)

A writer, scholar, editor, and co-founder of the National Association for the Advancement of Colored People (NAACP), William Edward Burghardt (W.E.B.) Du Bois inaugurated the modern civil rights movement, began the systematic development of black studies, was a catalyst in the development of the Pan-African movement, and was one of the most influential historians in late nineteenth- and early twentieth-century America. In addition to writing extensively on African American liberation and institutional racism, he edited *The Crisis*, the official magazine of the NAACP, for nearly a quarter-century and produced a number of works of sociology and history that were long ignored by white academia. His best-known book, *The Souls of Black Folk* (1903), is now regarded by many historians as no less influential than Harriet Beecher Stowe's antebellum novel *Uncle Tom's Cabin* (1852) in bringing social injustice to blacks to the forefront of American consciousness.

Early Life and Work

Born on February 23, 1868, in Great Barrington, Massachusetts, Du Bois was a self-described "mulatto" of African and French descent. A child of middle-class parents, raised in an integrated New England community, he encountered Jim Crow laws for the first time while attending Fisk University in Nashville, Tennessee, where he earned a bachelor's degree in 1888. Du Bois earned a second undergraduate degree in history from Harvard University in 1890, did two years of graduate work at the University of Berlin, and in 1895 became the first African American to be awarded a Ph.D. from Harvard, also in history. His doctoral dissertation, *The*

Suppression of the African Slave Trade to the United States, 1638–1870, was published the following year.

As an assistant instructor of sociology at the University of Pennsylvania in 1896–1897, Du Bois conducted groundbreaking research on an urban community whose results he published in *The Philadelphia Negro: A Social Study* (1899). Securing his place among leading African American scholars, the book exposed racial segregation, poverty, and moral crisis in the inner city and introduced his theory of "the talented tenth": that progress for the black community would come through the leadership of its most educated members.

It was his combination of scholarship, activism, and polemics as a professor of sociology and economics at the historically black Atlanta University (1897–1910) that brought Du Bois to national prominence. In 1903, he published *The Souls of Black Folk,* which opened with a bold declaration: "[T]he Problem of the Twentieth Century is the problem of the color-line," he wrote. In the book's 14 essays and sketches, Du Bois articulated a position against that of African American educator Booker T. Washington, who accepted an incremental approach to civil rights by emphasizing the importance of self-help, economic development, and technical training for blacks. In July 1905, Du Bois joined with several other African American civil rights activists in founding the Niagara Movement, which demanded an immediate end to all discrimination against blacks—another repudiation of Washington's conciliatory approach. The Niagara Movement finally was absorbed into the larger NAACP, which Du Bois helped found in February 1909. From the beginning of NAACP operations in 1910 until 1934, he served as a member of the board of directors, head of publicity and research, and editor of *The Crisis.*

Under Du Bois's leadership, the circulation of *The Crisis* increased from 10,000 copies in 1909 to 100,000 by 1919, giving him the opportunity to reach a much wider audience for his campaign against racial injustice. The magazine carried on a long-term crusade against lynching, with Du Bois hanging a sign from the publication's office window every time an African American was lynched. During World War I, he angered many of his colleagues by supporting the war effort and downplaying discrimination against African Americans in both military and civilian life.

The leading African American scholar and activist of his time, W.E.B. Du Bois advanced his increasingly radical views in *The Crisis*, the official NCAA journal he edited, and *The Souls of Black Folk* (1903), among other writings.

Later Causes and Writings

Du Bois's view of history emphasized the capacity of African Americans to take control of their own destiny. Although his political activities tended toward lobbying for reform and equal rights under the law, his legacy in many respects is more radical. He fought not only for civil rights for African Americans and independence from colonialism for Africans, but also for the broader democratization of American and Western civilization. As an advocate for the Pan-African movement, he attended the first international conference in London in 1900, where he was elected vice-president, and organized Pan-African congresses in 1919, 1921, 1923, and 1927. The Fifth Congress, in 1945, elected him chairman.

After a 10-year absence, Du Bois returned to the NAACP in 1944, though his openly radical politics and support for the international pacifist and antinuclear movements forced him to resign four years later and left him as a pariah in the African American community—not to mention the American public at large. As a target of McCarthyism in the 1950s, he faced trial as an agent of a foreign power; although the charges were later dismissed, Du Bois's passport was confiscated for eight years. After it was reinstated in 1961, he renounced his U.S. citizenship and joined the Communist Party to protest the repression of his civil liberties. Two years later, at age 95, Du Bois became a citizen of the West African nation of Ghana. He died there on August 27, 1963, one day before the March on Washington where the Reverend Martin Luther King, Jr., gave his historic "I Have a Dream" speech.

Du Bois's legacy in the fight for African American equality and the broader civil rights movement is embodied in his extensive writings. As a sociologist, historian, polemicist, novelist, and poet, he wrote 21 book-length works, edited 15 others, and published more than 100 essays and articles. In addition to *The Suppression of the African Slave Trade*, *The Philadelphia Negro*, and *The Souls of Black Folk*, his principal works include *John Brown* (1909), a sympathetic biography of the nineteenth-century antislavery radical; *Black Reconstruction in America* (1935), an economic history that illuminates the clash between the black and white working classes during the postbellum era; *Dusk of Dawn* (1940), subtitled "An Essay Toward an Autobiography of a Race Concept"; and *The Autobiography of W. E. Burghardt Du Bois* (1968). Of his six novels, the most notable is *Dark Princess: A Romance* (1928), on the themes of racial solidarity in the developing world and an international conspiracy for freedom. *Darkwater: Voices from Within the Veil* (1920) is a collection of essays and poetry; *The Negro* (1915) and *The Gift of Black Folk: Negroes in the Making of America* (1924) are two general histories of his people.

Said Dr. King of his predecessor in the civil rights movement, "History cannot ignore W.E.B. Du Bois, because history has to reflect truth. Du Bois was a tireless explorer and a gifted discoverer of social truths. . . . There were very few scholars who concerned themselves with honest study of the black man, and he sought to fill this immense void. The degree to which he succeeded disclosed the great dimensions of the man."

Matthew Quest, Annette Richardson, and Solomon Davidoff

◇◇◇

Chapter One, "Of Our Spiritual Strivings," *The Souls of Black Folk*, 1903

◇◇◇

In The Souls of Black Folk: Essays and Sketches, *a classic of African American literature, W.E.B. Du Bois explores black cultural tradition and argues passionately that the path to liberation lies in the leadership of an educated black elite. This view differed sharply from the philosophy of gradualism being advanced by African American leader Booker T. Washington, who emphasized technical training and self-help as the keys to achieving racial equality. In Chapter One, Du Bois introduces the recurring theme of "double consciousness." According to his theory, blacks in America face a profound challenge in having to reconcile their African cultural heritage with their Anglo-Saxon upbringing and education. This double-consciousness—"this sense of always looking at one's self through the eyes of others, of measuring one's soul by the tape of a world that looks on in amused contempt and pity"—is, he maintains, the source of an ongoing struggle of identity that has defined African American history and experience.*

> O water, voice of my heart, crying in the sand,
> All night long crying with a mournful cry,
> As I lie and listen, and cannot understand
> The voice of my heart in my side or the voice of the sea,
> O water, crying for rest, is it I, is it I?
> All night long the water is crying to me.
>
> Unresting water, there shall never be rest
> Till the last moon droop and the last tide fail,
> And the fire of the end begin to burn in the west;
> And the heart shall be weary and wonder and cry like the sea,
> All life long crying without avail,
> As the water all night long is crying to me.
>
> *ARTHUR SYMONS*

Between me and the other world there is ever an unasked question: unasked by some through feelings of delicacy; by others through the difficulty of rightly framing it. All, nevertheless, flutter round it. They approach me in a half-hesitant sort of way, eye me curiously or compassionately, and then, instead of saying directly, How does it feel to be a problem? they say, I know an excellent colored man in my town; or, I fought at Mechanicsville; or, Do not these Southern outrages make your blood boil? At these I smile, or am interested, or reduce the boiling to a simmer, as the occasion may require. To the real question, How does it feel to be a problem? I answer seldom a word.

And yet, being a problem is a strange experience, —peculiar even for one who has never been anything else, save perhaps in babyhood and in Europe. It is in the early days of rollicking boyhood that the revelation first bursts upon one, all in a day, as it were. I remember well when the shadow swept across me. I was a little thing, away up in the hills of New England, where the dark Housatonic winds between Hoosac and Taghkanic to the sea. In a wee wooden schoolhouse, something put it into the boys' and girls' heads to buy gorgeous visiting-cards—ten cents a package—and exchange. The exchange was merry, till one girl, a tall newcomer, refused my card, —refused it peremptorily, with a glance. Then it dawned upon me with a certain suddenness that I was different from the others; or like, mayhap, in heart and life and longing, but shut out from their world by a vast veil. I had thereafter no desire to tear down that veil, to creep through; I held all beyond it in common contempt, and lived above it in a region of blue sky and great wandering shadows. That sky was bluest when I could beat my mates at examination-time, or beat them at a foot-race, or even beat their stringy heads. Alas, with the years all this fine contempt began to fade; for the words I longed for, and all their dazzling opportunities, were theirs, not mine. But they should not keep these prizes, I said; some, all, I would wrest from them. Just how I would do it I could never decide: by reading law, by healing the sick, by telling the wonderful tales that swam in my head, —some way. With other black boys the strife was not so fiercely sunny: their youth shrunk into tasteless sycophancy, or into silent hatred of the pale world about them and mocking distrust of everything white; or wasted itself in a bitter cry, Why did God make me an outcast and a stranger in mine own house? The shades of the prison-house closed round about us all: walls strait and stubborn to the whitest, but relentlessly narrow, tall, and unscalable to sons of night who must plod darkly on in resignation, or beat unavailing palms against the stone, or steadily, half hopelessly, watch the streak of blue above.

After the Egyptian and Indian, the Greek and Roman, the Teuton and Mongolian, the Negro is a sort of seventh son, born with a veil, and gifted with second-sight in this American world, —a world which yields him no true self-consciousness, but only lets him see himself through the revelation of the other world. It is a peculiar sensation, this double-consciousness, this sense of always looking at one's self through the eyes of others, of measuring one's soul by the tape of a world that looks on in amused contempt and pity. One ever feels his twoness, —an American, a Negro; two souls, two thoughts, two unreconciled strivings; two warring ideals in one dark body, whose dogged strength alone keeps it from being torn asunder.

The history of the American Negro is the history of this strife, —this longing to attain self-conscious manhood, to merge his double self into a better and truer self. In this merging he wishes neither of the older selves to be lost. He would not Africanize America, for America has too much to teach the world and Africa. He would not bleach his Negro soul in a flood of white Americanism, for he knows that Negro blood has a message for the world. He simply wishes to make it possible for a man to be both a Negro and an American, without being cursed and spit upon by his fellows, without having the doors of Opportunity closed roughly in his face.

This, then, is the end of his striving: to be a co-worker in the kingdom of culture, to escape both death and isolation, to husband and use his best powers and his latent genius. These powers of body and mind have in the past been strangely wasted, dispersed, or forgotten. The shadow of a mighty Negro past flits through the tale of Ethiopia the Shadowy and of Egypt the Sphinx. Through history, the powers of single black men flash here and there like falling stars, and die sometimes before the world has rightly gauged their brightness. Here in America, in the few days since Emancipation, the black man's turning hither and thither in hesitant and doubtful striving has often made his very strength to lose effectiveness, to seem like absence of power, like weakness. And yet it is not weakness, —it is the contradiction of double aims. The double-aimed struggle of the black artisan—on the one hand to escape white contempt for a nation of mere hewers of wood and drawers of water, and on the other hand to plough and nail and dig for a poverty-stricken horde—could only result in making him a poor craftsman, for he had but half a heart in either cause. By the poverty and ignorance of his people, the Negro minister or doctor was tempted toward quackery and demagogy; and by the criticism of the other world, toward ideals that made him ashamed of his lowly tasks. The would-be black *savant* was confronted by the paradox that the knowledge his people needed was a twice-told tale to his white neighbors, while the knowledge which would teach the white world was Greek to his own flesh and blood. The innate love of harmony and beauty that set the ruder souls of his people a-dancing and a-singing raised but confusion and doubt in the soul of the black artist; for the beauty revealed to him was the soul-beauty of a race which his larger audience despised, and he could not articulate the message of another people. This waste of double aims, this seeking to satisfy two unreconciled ideals, has wrought sad havoc with the courage and faith and deeds of ten thousand thousand people, —has sent them often wooing false gods and invoking false means of salvation, and at times has even seemed about to make them ashamed of themselves.

Away back in the days of bondage they thought to see in one divine event the end of all doubt and disappointment; few men ever worshipped Freedom with half such unquestioning faith as did the American Negro for two centuries. To him, so far as he thought and dreamed, slavery was indeed the sum of all villainies, the cause of all sorrow, the root of all prejudice; Emancipation was the key to a promised land of sweeter beauty than ever stretched before the eyes of wearied Israelites. In song and exhortation swelled one refrain—Liberty; in his tears and curses the God he implored had Freedom in his right hand. At last it came, —suddenly, fearfully, like a dream. With one wild

carnival of blood and passion came the message in his own
plaintive cadences:—

"Shout, O children!
Shout, you're free!
For God has bought your liberty!"

Years have passed away since then, —ten, twenty, forty; forty years
of national life, forty years of renewal and development, and yet
the swarthy spectre sits in its accustomed seat at the Nation's feast.
In vain do we cry to this our vastest social problem:—

"Take any shape but that, and my firm nerves
Shall never tremble!"

The Nation has not yet found peace from its sins; the freedman
has not yet found in freedom his promised land. Whatever of
good may have come in these years of change, the shadow of
a deep disappointment rests upon the Negro people, —a disappointment all the more bitter because the unattained ideal was
unbounded save by the simple ignorance of a lowly people.
     The first decade was merely a prolongation of the vain search
for freedom, the boon that seemed ever barely to elude their
grasp, —like a tantalizing will-o'-the-wisp, maddening and
misleading the headless host. The holocaust of war, the terrors
of the Ku-Klux Klan, the lies of carpet-baggers, the disorgani-
zation of industry, and the contradictory advice of friends and
foes, left the bewildered serf with no new watchword beyond
the old cry for freedom. As the time flew, however, he began to
grasp a new idea. The ideal of liberty demanded for its attain-
ment powerful means, and these the Fifteenth Amendment gave
him. The ballot, which before he had looked upon as a visible
sign of freedom, he now regarded as the chief means of gaining
and perfecting the liberty with which war had partially endowed
him. And why not? Had not votes made war and emancipated
millions? Had not votes enfranchised the freedmen? Was anything impossible to a power that had done all this? A million

black men started with renewed zeal to vote themselves into the kingdom. So the decade flew away, the revolution of 1876 came, and left the half-free serf weary, wondering, but still inspired. Slowly but steadily, in the following years, a new vision began gradually to replace the dream of political power, —a powerful movement, the rise of another ideal to guide the unguided, another pillar of fire by night after a clouded day. It was the ideal of "book-learning"; the curiosity, born of compulsory ignorance, to know and test the power of the cabalistic letters of the white man, the longing to know. Here at last seemed to have been discovered the mountain path to Canaan; longer than the highway of Emancipation and law, steep and rugged, but straight, leading to heights high enough to overlook life.

Slowly but steadily, in the following years, a new vision began gradually to replace the dream of political power. . . . It was the ideal of "book-learning."

Up the new path the advance guard toiled, slowly, heavily, doggedly; only those who have watched and guided the faltering feet, the misty minds, the dull understandings, of the dark pupils of these schools know how faithfully, how piteously, this people strove to learn. It was weary work. The cold statistician wrote down the inches of progress here and there, noted also where here and there a foot had slipped or some one had fallen. To the tired climbers, the horizon was ever dark, the mists were often cold, the Canaan was always dim and far away. If, however, the vistas disclosed as yet no goal, no resting-place, little but flattery and criticism, the journey at least gave leisure for reflection and self-examination; it changed the child of Emancipation to the youth with dawning self-consciousness, self-realization, self-respect. In those sombre forests of his striving his own soul rose before him, and he saw himself, —darkly as through a veil; and yet he saw in himself some faint revelation of his power, of his mission. He began to have a dim feeling that, to attain his place in the world, he must be himself, and not another. For the first time he sought to analyze the burden he bore upon his back, that dead-weight of social degradation partially masked behind a half-named Negro problem. He felt his poverty; without a cent, without a home, without land, tools, or savings, he had entered into competition with rich, landed, skilled neighbors. To be a poor man is hard, but to be a poor race in a land of dollars is the very bottom of hardships. He felt the weight of his ignorance, —not simply of letters, but of life, of business, of the humanities; the accumulated sloth and shirking and awkwardness of decades and centuries shackled his hands and feet. Nor was his burden all poverty and ignorance. The red stain of bastardy, which two centuries of systematic legal defilement of Negro women had stamped upon his race, meant not only the loss of ancient African chastity, but also the hereditary weight of a mass of corruption from white adulterers, threatening almost the obliteration of the Negro home.

A people thus handicapped ought not to be asked to race with the world, but rather allowed to give all its time and thought to its own social problems. But alas! while sociologists gleefully count his bastards and his prostitutes, the very soul of the toiling, sweating black man is darkened by the shadow of a vast despair. Men call the shadow prejudice, and learnedly explain it as the natural defence of culture against barbarism, learning against ignorance, purity against crime, the "higher" against the "lower" races. To which the Negro cries Amen! and swears that to so much of this strange prejudice as is founded on just homage to civilization, culture, righteousness, and progress, he humbly bows and meekly does obeisance. But before that nameless prejudice that leaps beyond all this he stands helpless, dismayed, and well-nigh speechless; before that personal disrespect and mockery, the ridicule and systematic humiliation, the distortion of fact and wanton license of fancy, the cynical ignoring of the better and the boisterous welcoming of the worse, the all-pervading desire to inculcate disdain for everything black, from Toussaint to the devil, —before this there rises a sickening despair that would disarm and discourage any nation save that black host to whom "discouragement" is an unwritten word.

But the facing of so vast a prejudice could not but bring the inevitable self-questioning, self-disparagement, and lowering of ideals which ever accompany repression and breed in an atmosphere of contempt and hate. Whisperings and portents came home upon the four winds: Lo! we are diseased and dying, cried the dark hosts; we cannot write, our voting is vain; what need of education, since we must always cook and serve? And the Nation echoed and enforced this self-criticism, saying: Be content to be servants, and nothing more; what need of higher culture for half-men? Away with the black man's ballot, by force or fraud, —and behold the suicide of a race! Nevertheless, out of the evil came something of good, —the more careful adjustment of education to real life, the clearer perception of the Negroes' social responsibilities, and the sobering realization of the meaning of progress.

So dawned the time of *Sturm und Drang:* storm and stress to-day rocks our little boat on the mad waters of the world-sea; there is within and without the sound of conflict, the burning of body and rending of soul; inspiration strives with doubt, and faith with vain questionings. The bright ideals of the past, —physical freedom, political power, the training of brains and the training of hands, —all these in turn have waxed and waned, until even the last grows dim and overcast. Are they all wrong, —all false? No, not that, but each alone was over-simple and incomplete, —the dreams of a credulous race-childhood, or the fond imaginings of the other world which does not know and does not want to know our power. To be really true, all these ideals must be melted and welded into one. The training of the schools we need to-day more than ever, —the training of deft hands, quick eyes and ears, and above all the broader, deeper, higher culture of gifted minds and pure hearts. The power of the ballot we need in sheer self-defence, —else what shall save us from a second slavery? Freedom, too, the long-sought, we still seek, —the freedom of life and limb, the freedom to work and think, the freedom to love and aspire. Work, culture, liberty, —all these we need, not singly but together, not successively but together, each growing and aiding each, and all striving toward that vaster ideal that swims before the Negro people, the ideal of human brotherhood, gained through the unifying ideal of Race; the ideal of fostering and developing the traits and talents of the Negro, not in opposition to or contempt for other races, but rather in large conformity to the greater ideals of the American Republic, in order that some day on American soil two world-races may give each to each those characteristics both so sadly lack. We the darker ones come even now not altogether empty-handed: there are to-day no truer exponents of the pure human spirit of the Declaration of Independence than the American Negroes; there is no true American music but the wild sweet melodies of the Negro slave; the American fairy tales and folklore are Indian and African; and, all in all, we black men seem the sole oasis of simple faith and reverence in a dusty desert of dollars and smartness. Will America be poorer if she replace her brutal dyspeptic blundering with light-hearted but determined Negro humility? or her coarse and cruel wit with loving jovial good-humor? or her vulgar music with the soul of the Sorrow Songs?

Merely a concrete test of the underlying principles of the great republic is the Negro Problem, and the spiritual striving of the freedmen's sons is the travail of souls whose burden is almost beyond the measure of their strength, but who bear it in the name of an historic race, in the name of this the land of their fathers' fathers, and in the name of human opportunity.

And now what I have briefly sketched in large outline let me on coming pages tell again in many ways, with loving emphasis and deeper detail, that men may listen to the striving in the souls of black folk.

Sources: American Studies at the University of Virginia (http://xroads.virginia.edu); W.E.B. Du Bois, *The Souls of Black Folk: Essays and Sketches* (Chicago: A.C. McClurg & Co., 1903).

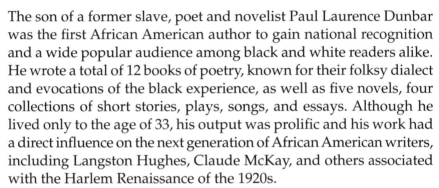

Dunbar, Paul Laurence

(1872–1906)

The son of a former slave, poet and novelist Paul Laurence Dunbar was the first African American author to gain national recognition and a wide popular audience among black and white readers alike. He wrote a total of 12 books of poetry, known for their folksy dialect and evocations of the black experience, as well as five novels, four collections of short stories, plays, songs, and essays. Although he lived only to the age of 33, his output was prolific and his work had a direct influence on the next generation of African American writers, including Langston Hughes, Claude McKay, and others associated with the Harlem Renaissance of the 1920s.

Dunbar was born in Dayton, Ohio, on June 27, 1872, the son of Joshua Dunbar, who had escaped to Canada before the Civil War and returned to the United States to fight for the Union, and Matilda Jane Dunbar, a laundry worker. Dunbar wrote his first poem at age 6 and recited an Easter poem publicly in church at age 9. A classmate and friend of future aviation pioneer Orville Wright, Dunbar served as editor-in-chief of the Dayton Central High School student newspaper, presided over the debating society, and wrote the class graduation song. While still in school, he contributed poems and sketches to the *Dayton Herald* and *West Side News*, a local paper published by Orville Wright, who had dropped out of school, and his brother Wilbur. Graduating in 1891, Dunbar hoped to become a lawyer but lacked the funds to pursue higher education and went to work as an elevator operator for $4 a week.

Defraying the costs himself, Dunbar published his first volume of poems, *Oak and Ivy*, in 1893. Later that year, he traveled to Chicago to write an article for the *Herald* about the World's Columbian Exposition. Taking a job as a latrine attendant, he remained in the

city and eventually obtained a position as clerk to former abolitionist Frederick Douglass, who was overseeing the Haitian Pavilion at
the fair.

Back in Dayton in 1895, Dunbar published his second verse collection, *Majors and Minors,* with the help of patrons from Toledo. In
June of the following year, William Dean Howells, America's most
prominent literary critic at the time, wrote an enthusiastic review
of the book for *Harper's Weekly,* and the endorsement effectively
launched Dunbar's career.

Lyrics of Lowly Life, a selection of 97 poems from his first two volumes, along with eight new poems and an introduction by Howells,
was published by Dodd, Mead and Company in 1896 and won near
universal acclaim. After returning from a reading tour in England,
Dunbar married teacher and writer Alice Ruth More and accepted
a position as a library assistant at the Library of Congress in Washington, D.C.

The years 1898–1903 were filled with more critical and popular
success. *Lippincott's Monthly Magazine* published Dunbar's first novel,
The Uncalled, in serial form in 1898. That same year, he produced
Folks from Dixie, a collection of 12 short stories; and his hit Broadway
musical, *Clorindy,* created with composer Will Marion Cook, opened
in June. By year's end, Dunbar had resigned his library position and
devoted himself full-time to writing.

In 1899, after publishing two more poetry collections, *Lyrics of
the Hearthside* and *Poems of Cabin and Field,* he embarked on another
reading tour but had to cut it short because of tuberculosis. While
convalescing in Denver, he wrote a Western novel titled *The Love
of Landry* (1900); another short-fiction collection, *The Strength of
Gideon and Other Stories* (1900); and two plays. Notable among
Dunbar's many works in the last five years of his life were *The
Sport of the Gods* (1902), a novel about the plight of urban blacks;
the poetry collections *Lyrics of Love and Laughter* (1903), *When
Malindy Sings* (1903), and *Lyrics of Sunshine and Shadow* (1905);
and another show with Cook, *In Dahomey* (1902), said to be the
first full-length Broadway musical created and performed entirely
by blacks. Dunbar died of tuberculosis at his home in Dayton on
February 9, 1906.

Carol E. Dietrich

◇◇◇

Selected Poems, 1896

◇◇◇

The two poems that follow appeared in Dunbar's first major collection,
Lyrics of Lowly Life *(1896). "Ode to Ethiopia" heralds black nation-
alist pride at a time when much of Africa was controlled by European
colonial powers but Ethiopia remained under native rule. And in the
year of* Plessy v. Ferguson, *in which the U.S. Supreme Court upheld
racial segregation in public facilities under the "separate but equal"
doctrine, Dunbar's poem "We Wear the Mask" describes the persona
of contented servility that hid the pain endured by former slaves and
other African Americans employed in such jobs as railway porters and
domestics.*

"Ode to Ethiopia"

> O Mother Race! to thee I bring
> This pledge of faith unwavering,
> This tribute to thy glory.
> I know the pangs which thou didst feel,
> When Slavery crushed thee with its heel,
> With thy dear blood all gory.
>
> Sad days were those—ah, sad indeed!
> But through the land the fruitful seed
> Of better times was growing.
> The plant of freedom upward sprung,
> And spread its leaves so fresh and young—
> Its blossoms now are blowing.
>
> On every hand in this fair land,
> Proud Ethiope's swarthy children stand
> Beside their fairer neighbor;
> The forests flee before their stroke,
> Their hammers ring, their forges smoke,—
> They stir in honest labour.

They tread the fields where honour calls;
Their voices sound through senate halls
In majesty and power.
To right they cling; the hymns they sing
Up to the skies in beauty ring,
And bolder grow each hour.

Be proud, my Race, in mind and soul;
Thy name is writ on Glory's scroll
In characters of fire.
High mid the clouds of Fame's bright sky
Thy banner's blazoned folds now fly,
And truth shall lift them higher.

Thou hast the right to noble pride,
Whose spotless robes were purified
By blood's severe baptism.
Upon thy brow the cross was laid,
And labour's painful sweat-beads made
A consecrating chrism.

No other race, or white or black,
When bound as thou wert, to the rack,
So seldom stooped to grieving;
No other race, when free again,
Forgot the past and proved them men
So noble in forgiving.

Go on and up! Our souls and eyes
Shall follow thy continuous rise;
Our ears shall list thy story
From bards who from thy root shall spring,
And proudly tune their lyres to sing
Of Ethiopia's glory.

"We Wear the Mask"

We wear the mask that grins and lies,
It hides our cheeks and shades our eyes,—
This debt we pay to human guile;
With torn and bleeding hearts we smile,
And mouth with myriad subtleties.

Why should the world be overwise,
In counting all our tears and sighs?
Nay, let them only see us, while
We wear the mask.

We smile, but, O great Christ, our cries
To thee from tortured souls arise.
We sing, but oh the clay is vile
Beneath our feet, and long the mile;
But let the world dream otherwise,
We wear the mask!

Sources: Paul Laurence Dunbar Web Site, University of Dayton (www.dunbarsite. org); P.L. Dunbar, *The Complete Poems of Paul Laurence Dunbar* (New York: Dodd, Mead and Company, 1913).

Howells, William Dean
(1837–1920)

A rare combination of author, editor, critic, and mentor to a generation of new writers, William Dean Howells is regarded by scholars as the father of American literary realism, making him perhaps the most influential man of letters of the Gilded Age and Progressive Era. The success of such contemporaries as Mark Twain, Bret Harte, and Henry James, and of such younger writers as Stephen Crane and Sarah Orne Jewett, was due in large measure to Howell's support and to his commentaries as editor of *The Atlantic Monthly* and as an independent literary critic. As a novelist in his own right, he engaged in the realistic depiction of life in industrialized urban America and examined attendant issues of commonsense morality and justice.

Howells was born in the small town of Martinsville (now Martin's Ferry), Ohio, on March 1, 1837. The son of an itinerant newspaper publisher and abolitionist, he began setting type for his father at a young age and read extensively in his father's home library. After serving for two years as a clerk in the State House of Representatives, Howells took a position in 1858 on the *Ohio State Journal,* for which he wrote short stories, poems, and translations.

The turning point in Howell's career came in 1860 with the publication of his campaign biography of Abraham Lincoln. With the money and reputation earned on that project, Howells traveled to New England to meet some of the leading literary lights of the time, including Henry Adams, Henry James, Nathaniel Hawthorne, Ralph Waldo Emerson, and Henry David Thoreau. His service to the Republican campaign also secured him the position of U.S. consul to Venice, Italy, where he served from 1861 to 1865. On Christmas Eve 1862, at the American Embassy in Paris, he was married to Elinor Mead, a sister of sculptor Larkin Goldsmith Mead and architect William Rutherford Mead.

Settling in Cambridge, Massachusetts, upon their return to the States, Howells began writing for several magazines and in 1866 accepted an assistant editor position at *The Atlantic Monthly*. He was named chief editor in 1871 and spent the next decade elevating the stature and broadening the readership of the magazine with stories by the likes of Twain, James, and Harte, some of whom became friends. The position offered Howells a unique role as an arbiter of American culture, which he used to promote the future of literary realism through both article selection and criticism.

Resigning from the *Atlantic* in 1881 to pursue independent writing, Howells incited what was called the Realism War with an 1882 article in *The Century* that defended the novels of Henry James; writers on both sides of the Atlantic engaged in vigorous debate over the merits of realistic versus romantic fiction as a mode of literary representation. In short succession thereafter, Howells published most of his own finest and best-known works of fiction. *A Modern Instance* (1882) went beyond the traditional romance novel in examining psychological and social disintegration amid the urbanization of post–Civil War America. *The Rise of Silas Lapham* (1885) and *A Hazard of New Fortunes* (1890), which Howells judged his best works of long fiction, were highly critical of the acquisitive and superficial quality of life in Gilded Age America. And in *A Traveler from Altruria* (1894), he created a utopian society in which people had outgrown those characteristics and valued humanity above material goods.

A staunch Republican in his younger years, Howells became increasingly radical in political outlook. He risked his reputation by siding publicly with the immigrant labor agitators and anarchists who had been imprisoned and hanged for their alleged role in the Haymarket affair of May 1886, asserting that they had been tried for their political views rather than for the crimes as charged. Other works of Howell's from this period, including scores of stories, plays, and essays, forthrightly examined contemporary issues of labor, class, race, and gender. He was elected as the first president of the American Academy of Arts and Letters in 1908 and was a founding member of the National Association for the Advancement of Colored People (NAACP) in 1909. By the end of his life on May 11, 1920, Howells was known as the "dean of American letters."

Wolfgang Hochbruck

See also: Crane, Stephen; James, Henry; Realism; Twain, Mark

XXX

Chapter 18, *Criticism and Fiction* (excerpt), 1891

XXXXXXXXXXXXXXXXXXXXXXXXXXXXXXXXXXXXXXXXXXXXXXXXXXX

As a literary critic, editor, and novelist in his own right, William Dean Howells was the foremost proponent of literary realism in America. His 1891 book Criticism and Fiction, *a collection of magazine articles and essays, represents a specific effort to define and describe his brand of "reticent realism." As Howells writes in Chapter 18, "Tests of Fiction," excerpted here, the first question to ask about a work of fiction is simply "Is it true— true to the motives, the impulses, the principles that shape the life of actual men and women?"*

[F]or my own part I will confess that I believe fiction in the past to have been largely injurious, as I believe the stage-play to be still almost wholly injurious, through its falsehood, its folly, its wantonness, and its aimlessness. It may be safely assumed that most of the novel-reading which people fancy an intellectual pastime is the emptiest dissipation, hardly more related to thought or the wholesome exercise of the mental faculties than opium-eating; in either case the brain is drugged, and left weaker and crazier for the debauch. If this may be called the negative result of the fiction habit, the positive injury that most novels work is by no means so easily to be measured in the case of young men whose character they help so much to form or deform, and the women of all ages whom they keep so much in ignorance of the world they misrepresent. Grown men have little harm from them, but in the other cases, which are the vast majority, they hurt because they are not true—not because they are malevolent, but because they are idle lies about human nature and the social fabric, which it behooves us to know and to understand, that we may deal justly with ourselves and with one another. One need not go so far as our correspondent, and trace to the fiction habit "whatever is wild and visionary, whatever is untrue, whatever is injurious," in one's life; bad as the fiction habit is it is probably not responsible for the whole sum of evil in its victims, and I believe that if the reader will use care in choosing from this fungus-growth with which the fields of literature teem every day, he may nourish himself as with the true mushroom, at no risk from the poisonous species.

The tests are very plain and simple, and they are perfectly infallible. If a novel flatters the passions, and exalts them above the principles, it is poisonous; it may not kill, but it will certainly injure; and this test will alone exclude an entire class of fiction, of which eminent examples will occur to all. Then the whole spawn of so-called unmoral romances, which imagine a world where the sins of sense are unvisited by the penalties following, swift or slow, but inexorably sure, in the real world, are deadly poison: these do kill. The novels that merely tickle our prejudices and lull our judgment, or that coddle our sensibilities or pamper our gross appetite for the marvellous, are not so fatal, but they are innutritious, and clog the soul with unwholesome vapors of all kinds. No doubt they too help to weaken the moral fibre, and make their readers indifferent to "plodding perseverance and plain industry," and to "matter-of-fact poverty and commonplace distress."

> *If a novel flatters the passions, and exalts them above the principles, it is poisonous; it may not kill, but it will certainly injure. . . .*

Without taking them too seriously, it still must be owned that the "gaudy hero and heroine" are to blame for a great deal of harm in the world. That heroine long taught by example, if not precept, that Love, or the passion or fancy she mistook for it, was the chief interest of a life, which is really concerned with a great many other things; that it was lasting in the way she knew it; that it was worthy of every sacrifice, and was altogether a finer thing than prudence, obedience, reason; that love alone was glorious and beautiful, and these were mean and ugly in comparison with it. More lately she has begun to idolize and illustrate Duty, and she is hardly less mischievous in this new role, opposing duty, as she did love, to prudence, obedience, and reason. The stock hero, whom, if we met him, we could not fail to see was a most deplorable person, has undoubtedly imposed himself upon the victims of the fiction habit as admirable. With him, too, love was and is the great affair, whether in its old romantic phase of chivalrous achievement or manifold suffering for love's sake, or its more recent development of the "virile," the bullying, and the brutal, or its still more recent agonies of self-sacrifice, as idle and useless as the moral experiences of the insane asylums. With his vain posturings and his ridiculous splendor he is really a painted barbarian, the prey of his passions and his delusions, full of obsolete ideals, and the motives and ethics of a savage, which the guilty author of his being does his best—or his worst—in spite of his own light and knowledge, to foist upon the reader as something generous and noble. I am not merely bringing this charge against that sort of fiction which is beneath literature and outside of it, "the shoreless lakes of ditch-water," whose miasms fill the air below the empyrean where the great ones sit; but I am accusing the work of some of the most famous, who have, in this instance or in that, sinned against the truth, which can alone exalt and purify men. I do not say that they have constantly done so, or even commonly done so; but that they have done so at all marks them as of the past, to be read with the due historical allowance for their epoch and their conditions. For I believe that, while inferior writers will and must continue to imitate them in their foibles and their errors, no one here after will be able to achieve greatness who is false to humanity, either in its facts or its duties. The light of civilization has already broken even upon the novel, and no conscientious man can now set about painting an image of life without perpetual question of the verity of his work, and without feeling bound to distinguish so clearly that no reader of his may be misled, between what is right and what is wrong, what is noble and what is base, what is health and what is perdition, in the actions and the characters he portrays.

The fiction that aims merely to entertain—the fiction that is to serious fiction as the opera-bouffe, the ballet, and the pantomime are to the true drama—need not feel the burden of this obligation so deeply; but even such fiction will not be gay or trivial to any reader's hurt, and criticism should hold it to account if it passes from painting to teaching folly.

I confess that I do not care to judge any work of the imagination without first of all applying this test to it. We must ask ourselves before we ask anything else, Is it true?—true to the motives, the impulses, the principles that shape the life of actual men and women? This truth, which necessarily includes the highest morality and the highest artistry—this truth given, the book cannot be wicked and cannot be weak; and without it all graces of style and feats of invention and cunning of construction are so many superfluities of naughtiness. It is well for the truth to have all these, and shine in them, but for falsehood they are merely meretricious, the bedizenment of the wanton; they atone for nothing, they count for nothing. But in fact they come naturally of truth, and grace it without solicitation; they are added unto it. In the whole range of fiction I know of no true picture of life—that is, of human nature—which is not also a masterpiece of literature, full of divine and natural beauty. It may have no touch or tint of this special civilization or of that; it had better have this local color well ascertained; but the truth is deeper and finer than aspects, and if the book is true to what men and women know of one another's souls it will be true enough, and it will be great and beautiful. It is the conception of literature as something apart from life, superfinely aloof, which makes it really unimportant to the great mass of mankind, without a message or a meaning for them; and it is the notion that a novel may be false in its portrayal of causes and effects that makes literary art contemptible even to those whom it amuses, that forbids them to regard the novelist as a serious or right-minded person. If they do not in some moment of indignation cry out against all novels, as my correspondent does, they remain besotted in the fume of the delusions purveyed to them, with no higher feeling for the author than such maudlin affection as the frequenter of an opium-joint perhaps knows for the attendant who fills his pipe with the drug.

Or, as in the case of another correspondent who writes that in his youth he "read a great many novels, but always regarded it as an amusement, like horse racing and card-playing," for which he had no time when he entered upon the serious business of life, it renders them merely contemptuous. His view of the matter may be commended to the brotherhood and sisterhood of novelists as full of wholesome if bitter suggestion; and I urge them not to dismiss it with high literary scorn as that of some Boeotian dull to the beauty of art. Refuse it as we may, it is still the feeling of the vast majority of people for whom life is earnest, and who find only a distorted and misleading likeness of it in our books. We may fold ourselves in our scholars' gowns, and close the doors of our studies, and affect to despise this rude voice; but we cannot shut it out. It comes to us from wherever men are at work, from wherever they are truly living, and accuses us of unfaithfulness, of triviality, of mere stage-play; and none of us can escape conviction except he prove himself worthy of his time—a time in which the great masters have brought literature back to life, and filled its ebbing veins with the red tides of reality. We cannot all equal them; we need not copy them; but we can all go to the sources of their inspiration and their power; and to draw from these no one need go far—no one need really go out of himself. . . .

I can hardly conceive of a literary self-respect in these days compatible with the old trade of make-believe, with the production of the kind of fiction which is too much honored by classification with card-playing and horse-racing. But let fiction cease to lie about life; let it portray men and women as they are, actuated by the motives and the passions in the measure we all know; let it leave off painting dolls and working them by springs and wires; let it show the different interests in their true proportions; let it forbear to preach pride and revenge, folly and insanity, egotism and prejudice, but frankly own these for what they are, in whatever figures and occasions they appear; let it not put on fine literary airs; let it speak the dialect, the language, that most Americans know—the language of unaffected people everywhere—and there can be no doubt of an unlimited future, not only of delightfulness but of usefulness, for it.

Sources: Project Gutenberg (www.gutenberg.org); W.D. Howells, *Criticism and Fiction* (New York: Harper and Brothers, 1891).

Huckleberry Finn

Adventures of Huckleberry Finn, Mark Twain's 1884 sequel to the popular *Adventures of Tom Sawyer* (1876)—both of which drew on Twain's youth along the Mississippi River in Hannibal, Missouri—is one of the most revered works of American literature and one of the most widely taught in the nation's classrooms. Ernest Hemingway famously wrote, "All modern American literature comes from one book by Mark Twain called *Huckleberry Finn.*" T.S. Eliot and H.L. Mencken are among the many who have called it a "masterpiece." According to one survey, the book is required reading in more than 70 percent of modern U.S. high schools.

Virtually from the moment it was published, however, *Huckleberry Finn* came under attack for its irreverence toward adult authority and religion, its use of vernacular, and, later, its purported racism. The public library in Concord, Massachusetts, banned the work as "rough, course, and inelegant, . . . more suitable to the slums than to intelligent, respectable people." The Brooklyn (NY) Public Library later barred the volume from its collection because the protagonist was dirty and used bad grammar; he "said 'sweat' when he should have said 'perspiration.'"

A satire of Southern society during the period before the Civil War, *Huckleberry Finn* is a first-person fictional narrative about the adventures of a teenage boy who escapes his abusive father and travels on a raft down the Mississippi River with a runaway slave named Jim. Their encounters with prejudice, hypocrisy, violence, and greed stand in rank contrast to their shared innocence and reflect the corrupting influences of the society they are attempting to escape. One of the hallmarks of the novel is Twain's (Huck's) use of dialect to relate the story—a literary technique that would pave the way for the likes of Stephen Crane, William Faulkner, Ernest Hemingway, and the African American writers of the Harlem Renaissance.

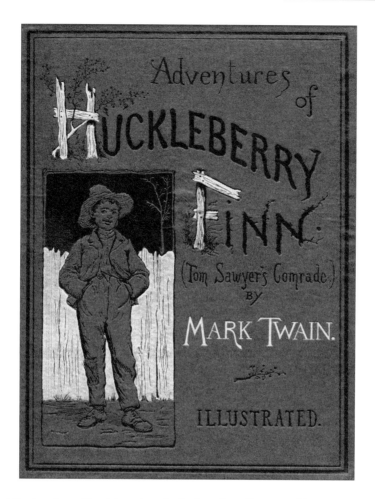

One of the iconic and best-loved works in American literature, Mark Twain's adventure novel and social satire *Huckleberry Finn* has also generated controversy since its first edition in 1884.

Although Twain's indictment of slavery and racial prejudice are as plain and as biting as his satire, the most persistent criticisms of *Huckleberry Finn* since the mid-twentieth century have alleged a "racist" aspect to the book. Such condemnation flared during the Civil Rights movement of the 1950s and 1960s, beginning with a 1957 statement from the NAACP objecting to the book's "racial slurs" and "belittling racial designations." The Board of Education in New York City removed Twain's classic from its list of approved books; a number of other school districts around the country followed suit in the succeeding decades. In the twenty-first century, according to various organizations, *Huckleberry Finn* still ranks among the most frequently challenged and censored books by U.S. schools and libraries.

Twain and his masterwork have faced their most vehement criticism for the frequent use of the "N-word" (nigger), which appears more than 200 times in the book. Educators, parents, and students themselves have pointed to the humiliation and insult of young African Americans for whom the racial epithet is reinforced repeatedly in class recitation or private reading. In one effort to spare readers from the racial slur and to restore the work to school reading lists, a new edition of *Huckleberry Finn* appeared in 2011 that replaced the N-word with the word "slave." That edition itself triggered a backlash of opposition; critics charged that such sanitization robs the work of its original character, ironic layering, and historical context.

Huckleberry Finn has faced criticism as well for perpetuating racial stereotypes through the portrayal of Jim as simple, childlike, and superstitious. Indeed, it has been said, Twain resorted to the stock imagery of the minstrel show in delineating the character. In reality, such criticism has found fewer and fewer proponents over the years, as most readers recognize the friendship, loyalty, and shared experience of freedom that emerges between Huck and Jim. The two have an affinity that cuts through all the hypocrisy and prejudice of society at large. Jim is an equal for whom Huck would "go to hell" rather than return to slavery. As the African American novelist Ralph Ellison would later observe,

> *Huckleberry Finn knew, as Mark Twain did, that Jim was not only a slave but a human being, a man who in some ways was to be envied, and who expressed his essential humanity in his desire for freedom, in his will to possess his own labor, in his loyalty and capacity for friendship. . . .*

Thus, it has been suggested, *Huckleberry Finn* ranks among the most powerful *anti*slavery, *anti*racist works in all of American literature.

Jeff Hacker

See also: Realism; Twain, Mark

◇◇

Chapter 12, *Adventures of Huckleberry Finn* (excerpt), 1884

◇◇

The relationship between young Huck and the runaway slave Jim, which evolves from wariness and distance to trust and friendship, lies at the heart of Mark Twain's commentary on slavery, race relations, and humanity in the Adventures of Huckleberry Finn. *The Mississippi River provides the setting for their shared adventure and a symbol of their quest for freedom. In Chapter 12, the raft becomes a kind of haven for Huck and Jim—a place of refuge, serenity, and camaraderie under the stars, removed from the dangers and evils on shore. They encounter the wreck of an old steamboat and debate whether to board it.*

It must a been close on to one o'clock when we got below the island at last, and the raft did seem to go mighty slow. If a boat was to come along we was going to take to the canoe and break for the Illinois shore; and it was well a boat didn't come, for we hadn't ever thought to put the gun in the canoe, or a fishing-line, or anything to eat. We was in ruther too much of a sweat to think of so many things. It warn't good judgment to put *everything* on the raft.

If the men went to the island I just expect they found the camp fire I built, and watched it all night for Jim to come. Anyways, they stayed away from us, and if my building the fire never fooled them it warn't no fault of mine. I played it as low down on them as I could.

When the first streak of day began to show we tied up to a towhead in a big bend on the Illinois side, and hacked off cottonwood branches with the hatchet, and covered up the raft with them so she looked like there had been a cave-in in the bank there. A towhead is a sandbar that has cottonwoods on it as thick as harrow-teeth.

We had mountains on the Missouri shore and heavy timber on the Illinois side, and the channel was down the Missouri shore at that place, so we warn't afraid of anybody running across us. We laid there all day, and watched the rafts and steamboats spin down the Missouri shore, and up-bound steamboats fight the big river in the middle. I told Jim all about the time I had jabbering with that woman; and Jim said she was a smart one, and if she was to start after us herself she wouldn't set down and watch a camp fire—no, sir, she'd fetch a dog. Well, then, I said, why couldn't she tell her husband to fetch a dog? Jim said he bet she did think of it by the time the men was ready to start, and he believed they must a gone up-town to get a dog and so they lost all that time, or else we wouldn't be here on a towhead sixteen or seventeen mile below the village—no, indeedy, we would be in that same old town again. So I said I didn't care what was the reason they didn't get us as long as they didn't.

When it was beginning to come on dark we poked our heads out of the cottonwood thicket, and looked up and down and across; nothing in sight; so Jim took up some of the top planks of the raft and built a snug wigwam to get under in blazing weather and rainy, and to keep the things dry. Jim made a floor for the wigwam, and raised it a foot or more above the level of the raft, so now the blankets and all the traps was out of reach of steamboat waves. Right in the middle of the wigwam we made a layer of dirt about five or six inches deep with a frame around it for to hold it to its place; this was to build a fire on in sloppy weather or chilly; the wigwam would keep it from being seen. We made an extra steering-oar, too, because one of the others might get broke on a snag or something. We fixed up a short forked stick to hang the old lantern on, because we must always light the lantern whenever we see a steamboat coming down-stream, to keep from getting run over; but we wouldn't have to light it for up-stream boats unless we see we was in what they call a "crossing"; for the river was pretty high yet, very low banks being still a little under water; so up-bound boats didn't always run the channel, but hunted easy water.

This second night we run between seven and eight hours, with a current that was making over four mile an hour. We catched fish and talked, and we took a swim now and then to keep off sleepiness. It was kind of solemn, drifting down the big, still river, laying on our backs looking up at the stars, and we didn't ever feel like talking loud, and it warn't often that we laughed—only a little kind of a low chuckle. We had mighty good weather as a general thing, and nothing ever happened to us at all—that night, nor the next, nor the next.

Every night we passed towns, some of them away up on black hillsides, nothing but just a shiny bed of lights; not a house could you see. The fifth night we passed St. Louis, and it was like the whole world lit up. In St. Petersburg they used to say there was twenty or thirty thousand people in St. Louis, but I never believed it till I see that wonderful spread of lights at two o'clock that still night. There warn't a sound there; everybody was asleep.

Every night now I used to slip ashore towards ten o'clock at some little village, and buy ten or fifteen cents' worth of meal or bacon or other stuff to eat; and sometimes I lifted a chicken that warn't roosting comfortable, and took him along. Pap always said, take a chicken when you get a chance, because if you don't want him yourself you can easy find somebody that does, and a good deed ain't ever forgot. I never see pap when he didn't want the chicken himself, but that is what he used to say, anyway.

Mornings before daylight I slipped into cornfields and borrowed a watermelon, or a mushmelon, or a punkin, or some new corn, or things of that kind. Pap always said it warn't no harm to borrow things if you was meaning to pay them back some time; but the widow said it warn't anything but a soft name for stealing, and no decent body would do it. Jim said he reckoned the widow was partly right and pap was partly right; so the best way would be for us to pick out two or three things from the list and say we wouldn't borrow them any more—then he reckoned it wouldn't be no harm to borrow the others. So we talked it over all one night, drifting along down the river, trying to make up our minds whether to drop the watermelons, or the cantelopes, or the mushmelons, or what. But towards daylight we got it all settled satisfactory, and concluded to drop crabapples and p'simmons. We warn't feeling just right before that, but it was all comfortable now. I was glad the way it come out, too, because crabapples ain't ever good, and the p'simmons wouldn't be ripe for two or three months yet.

We shot a water-fowl now and then that got up too early in the morning or didn't go to bed early enough in the evening. Take it all round, we lived pretty high.

The fifth night below St. Louis we had a big storm after midnight, with a power of thunder and lightning, and the rain poured down in a solid sheet. We stayed in the wigwam and let the raft take care of itself. When the lightning glared out we could see a big straight river ahead, and high, rocky bluffs on both sides. By and by says I, "Hel-LO, Jim, looky yonder!" It was a steamboat that had killed herself on a rock. We was drifting straight down for her. The lightning showed her very distinct. She was leaning over, with part of her upper deck above water, and you could see every little chimbly-guy clean and clear, and a chair by the big bell, with an old slouch hat hanging on the back of it, when the flashes come.

Well, it being away in the night and stormy, and all so mysterious-like, I felt just the way any other boy would a felt when I see that wreck laying there so mournful and lonesome in the middle of the river. I wanted to get aboard of her and slink around a little, and see what there was there. So I says:

"Le's land on her, Jim."

But Jim was dead against it at first. He says:

"I doan' want to go fool'n 'long er no wrack. We's doin' blame' well, en we better let blame' well alone, as de good book says. Like as not dey's a watchman on dat wrack."

"Watchman your grandmother," I says; "there ain't nothing to watch but the texas and the pilot-house; and do you reckon anybody's going to resk his life for a texas and a pilot-house such a night as this, when it's likely to break up and wash off down the river any minute?" Jim couldn't say nothing to that, so he didn't try. "And besides," I says, "we might borrow something worth having out of the captain's stateroom. Seegars, I bet you—and cost five cents apiece, solid cash. Steamboat captains is always rich, and get sixty dollars a month, and THEY don't care a cent what a thing costs, you know, long as they want it. Stick a candle in your pocket; I can't rest, Jim, till we give her a rummaging. Do you reckon Tom Sawyer would ever go by this thing? Not for pie, he wouldn't. He'd call it an adventure—that's what he'd call it; and he'd land on that wreck if it was his last act. And wouldn't he throw style into it?—wouldn't he spread himself, nor nothing? Why, you'd think it was Christopher C'lumbus discovering Kingdom-Come. I wish Tom Sawyer WAS here."

Jim he grumbled a little, but give in. He said we mustn't talk any more than we could help, and then talk mighty low. The lightning showed us the wreck again just in time, and we fetched the stabboard derrick, and made fast there.

Sources: Literature.org: The Online Literature Library (www.literature.org); Mark Twain, *Adventures of Huckleberry Finn (Tom Sawyer's Comrade)* (New York: Charles L. Webster and Company, 1885).

James, Henry

(1843–1916)

Novelist, short-story writer, essayist, and playwright Henry James was a leading exponent of nineteenth-century literary realism and is widely regarded as the most accomplished American writer of his generation. While hewing to the realist principle of depicting events, individuals, and society "as they really are," James brought a unique refinement to his writing, marked by the complexity of his characterization and the psychological subtleties revealed in his subjects. Although he relocated to Europe and became a British subject late in life, he remained essentially American in his outlook. The theme of many of his novels is the conflict between the resolute but naïve character of his American protagonists and the more sophisticated society and culture of the Old World. James's fiction is prized for its subtle analysis of the human psyche, meticulous literary craft, and insights into the bond developing between America and Europe.

Henry James was born in New York City on April 15, 1843, to prominent and wealthy parents: theologian Henry James, Sr., and Mary Walsh James, the daughter of a cotton merchant. He was raised in a family in which a high value was placed on learning. Nathaniel Hawthorne, Ralph Waldo Emerson, and Henry David Thoreau, friends of his father, were regular visitors to the James home. The family spent a number of years in the capitals of Europe, and Henry and his four brothers and sisters were privately tutored in foreign languages, literature, and the classics. His older brother was the psychologist and pragmatic philosopher William James.

James entered Harvard University at age 19 to study law, but he soon became enamored with the writings of French novelist Honoré de Balzac, a founder of European realism who demonstrated how social and economic forces alter human behavior. James was later

Henry James, depicted here by the great portrait artist John Singer Sargent, spearheaded American literary realism with novels of refined style and keen psychological insight.

influenced by such other Europeans as Gustave Flaubert, another seminal figure in the realist movement; Émile Zola, known as a practitioner of naturalist fiction; and the Russian realist Ivan Turgenev. With a similar sense of literary and social mission, James turned to writing as a profession. And he would be prolific. He went on to produce a total of 22 novels, 112 short stories, 15 plays, seven travel books, and three autobiographical volumes. He also wrote the equivalent of about 10 volumes of critical essays, which appeared in the *Nation, New York Tribune, Atlantic Monthly,* and other leading periodicals of the day.

James developed his craft during an era in which some American intellectuals despaired that the nation's culture would devolve into the popular culture of ordinary citizens as opposed to the high culture of sophisticated artists. He lamented what, in some respects, many countrymen celebrated in America—that it had "no sovereign, no court, no personal loyalty, no church, no diplomatic service, nor old country houses, nor ivied ruins, nor great universities."

Despite his youthful experiences in Europe and his foreign literary influences, James established his career in the United States. He published his first short story, "A Tragedy of Errors" (1864), there and contributed regularly to the *Nation* and *Atlantic Monthly* into the early 1870s. The editor of the latter publication, William Dean Howells, became a champion of his work and a lifelong friend. It was not until settling in England in 1876, however, that James began producing the realist psychological novels for which he is best known. Among these are *The American* (1877), *The Europeans* (1878), *Washington Square* (1880), *The Portrait of a Lady* (1881), *The Bostonians* (1886), *The Wings of the Dove* (1902), and *The Ambassadors* (1903). Other prominent works include the novellas *Daisy Miller* (1878) and *The Turn of the Screw* (1898), the extended critical essay *Hawthorne* (1879), and three autobiographical volumes, *A Small Boy and Others* (1913), *Notes of a Son and Brother* (1914), and *The Middle Years* (1917, posthumous).

Successful in business and highly sociable, James was welcomed in the great houses of Britain and the continent, where he befriended many of Europe's literary and cultural elite. He lived in Europe nearly continuously after the mid-1870s and did not visit the United States for nearly two decades after 1883. He lived the last nine years of his life at Lamb House in Rye, East Sussex, England, and became a British subject in 1915 to protest U.S. neutrality during World War I in Europe.

Henry James died of pneumonia in London on February 28, 1916. His ashes were returned for burial in Cambridge, Massachusetts, where his gravestone is inscribed as follows: "Novelist—Citizen of Two Countries, Interpreter of His Generation On Both Sides Of The Sea." In 1976, a memorial stone in his honor was placed in the Poets' Corner of Westminster Abbey in London.

Hettie Williams and Jeff Hacker

See also: Howells, William Dean; Realism

◇◇◇

Chapter One, *The American* (excerpt), 1877

◇◇◇

Set in France in 1868, The American *is Henry James's first novel about the cultural divide between the Old World and the New World—a recurring subject of his major works of fiction.* The American *tells the story of a wealthy but unsophisticated Yankee businessman named Christopher Newman whose money and success cannot buy him admission into French society. The opening scene, in which Newman meets an attractive young artist at the Louvre in Paris and offers to buy one of her paintings, sets the tone and theme of this novel of manners and social comedy. For its depiction of the clash of cultures,* The American *has been called the "first international novel."*

On a brilliant day in May, in the year 1868, a gentleman was reclining at his ease on the great circular divan which at that period occupied the centre of the Salon Carre, in the Museum of the Louvre. This commodious ottoman has since been removed, to the extreme regret of all weak-kneed lovers of the fine arts, but the gentleman in question had taken serene possession of its softest spot, and, with his head thrown back and his legs outstretched, was staring at Murillo's beautiful moon-borne Madonna in profound enjoyment of his posture. He had removed his hat, and flung down beside him a little red guide-book and an opera-glass. The day was warm; he was heated with walking, and he repeatedly passed his handkerchief over his forehead, with a somewhat wearied gesture. And yet he was evidently not a man to whom fatigue was familiar; long, lean, and muscular, he suggested the sort of vigor that is commonly known as "toughness." But his exertions on this particular day had been of an unwonted sort, and he had performed great physical feats which left him less jaded than his tranquil stroll through the Louvre. He had looked out all the pictures to which an asterisk was affixed in those formidable pages of fine print in his Badeker; his attention had been strained and his eyes dazzled, and he had sat down with an aesthetic headache. He had looked, moreover, not only at all the pictures, but at all the copies that were going forward around them, in the hands of those innumerable young women in irreproachable toilets who devote themselves, in France, to the propagation of masterpieces, and if the truth must be told, he had often admired the copy much more than the original. His physiognomy would have sufficiently indicated that he was a shrewd and capable fellow, and in truth he had often sat up all night over a bristling bundle of accounts, and heard the cock crow without a yawn. But Raphael and Titian and Rubens were a new kind of arithmetic, and they inspired our friend, for the first time in his life, with a vague self-mistrust.

An observer with anything of an eye for national types would have had no difficulty in determining the local origin of this undeveloped connoisseur, and indeed such an observer might have felt a certain humorous relish of the almost ideal completeness with which he filled out the national mould. The gentleman on the divan was a powerful specimen of an American. But he was not only a fine American; he was in the first place, physically, a fine man. He appeared to possess that kind of health and strength which, when found in perfection, are the most impressive—the physical capital which the owner does nothing to "keep up." If he was a muscular Christian, it was quite without knowing it. If it was necessary to walk to a remote spot, he walked, but he had never known himself to "exercise." He had no theory with regard to cold bathing or the use of Indian clubs; he was neither an oarsman, a rifleman, nor a fencer—he had never had time for these amusements—and he was quite unaware that the saddle is recommended for certain forms of indigestion. He was by inclination a temperate man; but he had supped the night before his visit to the Louvre at the Cafe Anglais—some one had told him it was an experience not to be omitted—and he had slept none the less the sleep of the just. His usual attitude and carriage were of a rather relaxed and lounging kind, but when under a special inspiration, he straightened himself, he looked like a grenadier on parade. He never smoked. He had been assured—such things are said—that cigars were excellent for the health, and he was quite capable of believing it; but he knew as little about tobacco as about homeopathy. He had a very well-formed head, with a shapely, symmetrical balance of the frontal and the occipital development, and a good deal of straight, rather dry brown hair. His complexion was brown, and his nose had a bold well-marked arch. His eye was of a clear, cold gray, and save for a rather abundant mustache he was clean-shaved. He had the flat jaw and sinewy neck which are frequent in the American type; but the traces of national origin are a matter of expression even more than of feature, and it was in this respect that our friend's countenance was supremely eloquent. The discriminating observer we have been supposing might, however, perfectly have measured its expressiveness, and yet have been at a loss to describe it. It had that typical vagueness which is not vacuity, that blankness which is not simplicity, that look of being committed to nothing in particular, of standing in an attitude of general hospitality to the chances of life, of being very much at one's own disposal so characteristic of many American faces. It was our friend's eye that chiefly told his story; an eye in which innocence and experience were singularly blended. It was full of contradictory suggestions, and though it was by no means the glowing orb of a hero of romance, you could find in it almost anything you looked for. Frigid and yet friendly, frank yet cautious, shrewd yet credulous, positive yet skeptical, confident yet shy, extremely intelligent and extremely good-humored, there was something vaguely defiant in its concessions, and something profoundly reassuring in its reserve. The cut of this gentleman's mustache, with the two premature wrinkles in the cheek above it, and the fashion of his garments, in which an exposed shirt-front and a cerulean cravat played perhaps an obtrusive part, completed the conditions of his identity. We have approached him, perhaps, at a not especially favorable moment; he is by no means sitting for his portrait. But listless as he lounges there, rather baffled on the aesthetic question, and guilty of the damning fault (as we have lately discovered it to be) of confounding the merit of the artist with that of his work (for he admires the squinting Madonna of the young lady with the boyish coiffure, because he thinks the young lady herself uncommonly taking), he is a sufficiently promising acquaintance. Decision, salubrity, jocosity, prosperity, seem to hover within his call; he is evidently a practical man, but the idea in his case, has undefined and mysterious boundaries, which invite the imagination to bestir itself on his behalf.

As the little copyist proceeded with her work, she sent every now and then a responsive glance toward her admirer. The cultivation of the fine arts appeared to necessitate, to her mind, a great deal of byplay, a great standing off with folded arms and head drooping from side to side, stroking of a dimpled chin with a dimpled hand, sighing and frowning and patting of the foot, fumbling in disordered tresses for wandering hair-pins. These performances were accompanied by a restless glance, which lingered longer than elsewhere upon the gentleman we have described. At last he rose abruptly, put on his hat, and approached the young lady. He placed himself before her picture and looked at it for some moments, during which she pretended to be quite unconscious of his inspection. Then, addressing her with the single word which constituted the strength of his French vocabulary, and holding up one finger in a manner which appeared to him to illuminate his meaning, "Combien?" he abruptly demanded.

The artist stared a moment, gave a little pout, shrugged her shoulders, put down her palette and brushes, and stood rubbing her hands.

"How much?" said our friend, in English. "Combien?"

"Monsieur wishes to buy it?" asked the young lady in French.

"Very pretty, splendide. Combien?" repeated the American.

"It pleases monsieur, my little picture? It's a very beautiful subject," said the young lady.

"The Madonna, yes; I am not a Catholic, but I want to buy it. Combien? Write it here." And he took a pencil from his pocket and showed her the fly-leaf of his guide-book. She stood looking at him and scratching her chin with the pencil. "Is it not for sale?" he asked. And as she still stood reflecting, and looking at him with an eye which, in spite of her desire to treat this avidity of patronage as a very old story, betrayed an almost touching incredulity, he was afraid he had offended her. She simply trying to look indifferent, and wondering how far she might go. "I haven't made a mistake—pas insulte, no?" her interlocutor continued. "Don't you understand a little English?"

The young lady's aptitude for playing a part at short notice was remarkable. She fixed him with her conscious, perceptive eye and asked him if he spoke no French. Then, "Donnez!" she said briefly, and took the open guide-book. In the upper corner of the fly-leaf she traced a number, in a minute and extremely neat hand. Then she handed back the book and took up her palette again.

Our friend read the number: "2,000 francs." He said nothing for a time, but stood looking at the picture, while the copyist began actively to dabble with her paint. "For a copy, isn't that a good deal?" he asked at last. "Pas beaucoup?"

The young lady raised her eyes from her palette, scanned him from head to foot, and alighted with admirable sagacity upon exactly the right answer. "Yes, it's a good deal. But my copy has remarkable qualities, it is worth nothing less."

The gentleman in whom we are interested understood no French, but I have said he was intelligent, and here is a good chance to prove it. He apprehended, by a natural instinct, the meaning of the young woman's phrase, and it gratified him to think that she was so honest. Beauty, talent, virtue; she combined everything! "But you must finish it," he said. "FINISH, you know;" and he pointed to the unpainted hand of the figure.

"Oh, it shall be finished in perfection; in the perfection of perfections!" cried mademoiselle; and to confirm her promise, she deposited a rosy blotch in the middle of the Madonna's cheek.

But the American frowned. "Ah, too red, too red!" he rejoined. "Her complexion," pointing to the Murillo, "is—more delicate."

"Delicate? Oh, it shall be delicate, monsieur; delicate as Sevres biscuit. I am going to tone that down; I know all the secrets of my art. And where will you allow us to send it to you? Your address?"

"My address? Oh yes!" And the gentleman drew a card from his pocket-book and wrote something upon it. Then hesitating a moment he said, "If I don't like it when it it's finished, you know, I shall not be obliged to take it."

The young lady seemed as good a guesser as himself. "Oh, I am very sure that monsieur is not capricious," she said with a roguish smile.

"Capricious?" And at this monsieur began to laugh. "Oh no, I'm not capricious. I am very faithful. I am very constant. Comprenez?"

"Monsieur is constant; I understand perfectly. It's a rare virtue. To recompense you, you shall have your picture on the first possible day; next week—as soon as it is dry. I will take the card of monsieur." And she took it and read his name: "Christopher Newman." Then she tried to repeat it aloud, and laughed at her bad accent. "Your English names are so droll!"

"Droll?" said Mr. Newman, laughing too. "Did you ever hear of Christopher Columbus?"

"Bien sur! He invented America; a very great man. And is he your patron?"

"My patron?"

"Your patron-saint, in the calendar."

"Oh, exactly; my parents named me for him."

"Monsieur is American?"

"Don't you see it?" monsieur inquired.

"And you mean to carry my little picture away over there?" and she explained her phrase with a gesture.

"Oh, I mean to buy a great many pictures—beaucoup, beaucoup," said Christopher Newman.

"The honor is not less for me," the young lady answered, "for I am sure monsieur has a great deal of taste."

Sources: Project Gutenberg (www.gutenberg.org); Henry James, *The American* (Boston: James R. Osgood and Company, 1877).

London, Jack
(1876–1916)

One of the most prolific and successful American writers of the early twentieth century—producing more than 50 novels and hundreds of short stories and nonfiction pieces—Jack London is best known for his novels of conflict, adventure, and the struggle to survive. Among these are such enduringly popular works as *The Call of the Wild* (1903), *The Sea-Wolf* (1904), and *White Fang* (1906), all prototypes of the naturalistic movement in American literature. A child of poverty, London dramatized his concern for social outcasts in both his fiction and his nonfiction, promoting at once a philosophy of radical socialism and the spirit of individualism. His own life of adventure provided the raw material for many of his books, much as his reading provided the philosophical underpinnings.

He was born John "Jack" Griffith Chaney in San Francisco on January 12, 1876. An illegitimate child, he was raised in nearby Oakland by his mother, Flora Wellman, and stepfather, John London. During his teenage years, the future writer worked at a variety of jobs that spurred his sense of adventure—pirating oysters, chasing maritime poachers in San Francisco Harbor, and sailing the Pacific Ocean as a deckhand on a sealing ship. He also spent endless hours reading in the Oakland Public Library.

At age 17, London embarked on a journey across America as a hobo, the details of which he chronicled in an autobiographical memoir, *The Road* (1907). Along the way, he joined the West Coast contingent of Coxey's Army, a mass of unemployed workers who marched on Washington, D.C., in 1894 to demand jobs during the economic depression then sweeping the country. London never actually made it to Washington—he spent 30 days in jail for vagrancy—but it was on this journey that he became acquainted with socialism. Upon returning to Oakland at age 19 to attend high school, he became an

A lifelong adventurer and proponent of leftist social philosophy, Jack London achieved both popular success in his time and enduring critical acclaim for his novels and short stories about the struggle for survival against the forces of nature.

active member of the Socialist Labor Party. His letter-writing campaign to local newspapers and his street-corner speeches earned him the nickname "Boy Socialist of Oakland."

London entered the University of California, Berkeley, in the fall of 1896, but financial circumstances, a hunger for adventure, and the desire to become a writer brought an end to his college education after one semester. In July 1897, he headed off to the Yukon with his brother-in-law to take part in the Klondike Gold Rush. Although he never discovered gold, his year in the Far North provided the raw material—setting, experiences, and theme of "man versus nature"—for his first successful short stories and his most beloved novels. Despite a bout with scurvy that left permanent aftereffects, London's time in the Far North also gave him a chance to study the works of German political philosopher Karl Marx and English naturalist Charles Darwin, whose insights into social justice and the struggle for survival would come to permeate his own writing.

Upon returning to California, London resolved to earn his livelihood from writing—a struggle described in his later auto-biographical novel *Martin Eden* (1909). Disciplined in his craft, he tried to work every morning and produce at least 1,000 words a day. A boom in mass-circulation magazine publishing at the turn of the century (resulting from advances in printing technology and cheaper distributions costs due to the spread of railroads) coincided with London's outburst of literary energy, providing a perfect venue for his broad-appeal short fiction. By 1902, he had published three volumes of stories and had established his career and reputation.

In 1903, London sold the rights to *The Call of the Wild* in both serial magazine form and book form. That work, along with its sequel, *White Fang*, and *The Sea-Wolf*, a philosophical adventure novel about an amoral ship captain—all within a three-year period—brought him lasting fame and unprecedented popularity. That fame, it has been noted, was in no small measure a function of another development in modern American society: the birth of mass-market print advertising and promotional marketing. More overtly political than his three blockbuster novels, and far less successful commercially, was *The Iron Heel* (1907), a broadside attack on capitalism and prescient forecast of the rise of fascism. *John Barleycorn* (1913) was an autobiographical memoir about alcoholism and his struggle to overcome it.

In addition to writing fiction, London served as a war correspondent in the Far East during the Russo-Japanese War in 1904 and in Mexico during the Villa-Carranza revolt in 1914. Following San Francisco's great earthquake and fire in April 1906, London and his second wife, Charmian, traveled into the city from their ranch in Glen Ellen, Sonoma County, to survey the damage. Although he vowed never to include the disaster in his work, he did produce a 2,500-word account of it for *Collier's Magazine*; "San Francisco is gone," he wrote. In the aftermath, he and Charmian spent two years sailing the Pacific in his custom-crafted schooner *Snark* to study Polynesian culture and tradition for future books. In the process, they popularized Hawaii and the Pacific Islands as tourist destinations.

Always looking for new projects and opportunities, London was among the first major writers to work in the motion-picture industry; *The Sea-Wolf* provided the raw material for the first full-length American feature film in 1914. He also broke ground by lending his name and image to several commercial endorsements, including ones for men's clothing and fruit juice.

London's darkest hour arrived on August 22, 1913, when Wolf House, the dream home he spent four years building, burned to the ground the night before he was to occupy it. The incident devastated him both emotionally and financially. At age 40, plagued by kidney disease and other ailments, London died at his California ranch on November 22, 1916; according to some accounts, he took a fatal dose of morphine.

Gavin J. Wilk and Brenda K. Jackson

See also: Naturalism

Chapter Two, "The Law of Club and Fang," *The Call of the Wild*, 1903

Jack London's hit adventure novel The Call of the Wild, *which has remained continuously in print from the first edition in 1903 to the present day, is the story of a domesticated California ranch dog named Buck who is stolen from his owner, transported to the Klondike, and forced to learn to survive as a sled dog. Dramatically recounting the struggles of dogs and men against the forces of nature, each other, and the primal instincts within themselves, the novel also operates as an allegory for the broader struggle between civilization and savagery. Chapter Two describes Buck's shocking first days in the wild and his first experiences with the other dogs (Curly, Spitz, Dave, and the rest of the team) and their masters (Francois and Perrault).*

Buck's first day on the Yea beach was like a nightmare. Every hour was filled with shock and surprise. He had been suddenly jerked from the heart of civilization and flung into the heart of things primordial. No lazy, sun-kissed life was this, with nothing to do but loaf and be bored. Here was neither peace, nor rest, nor a moment's safety. All was confusion and action, and every moment life and limb were in peril. There was imperative need to be constantly alert; for these dogs and men were not town dogs and men. They were savages, all of them, who knew no law but the law of club and fang.

He had never seen dogs fight as these wolfish creatures fought, and his first experience taught him an unforgettable lesson. It is true, it was a vicarious experience, else he would not have lived to profit by it. Curly was the victim. They were camped near the log store, where she, in her friendly way, made advances to a husky dog the size of a full-grown wolf, though not half so large as she. There was no warning, only a leap in like a flash, a metallic clip of teeth, a leap out equally swift, and Curly's face was ripped open from eye to jaw.

It was the wolf manner of fighting, to strike and leap away; but there was more to it than this. Thirty or forty huskies ran to the spot and surrounded the combatants in an intent and silent circle. Buck did not comprehend that silent intentness, nor the eager way with which they were licking their chops. Curly rushed her antagonist, who struck again and leaped aside. He met her next rush with his chest, in a peculiar fashion that tumbled her off her feet. She never regained them. This was what the onlooking huskies had waited for. They closed in upon her, snarling and yelping, and she was buried, screaming with agony, beneath the bristling mass of bodies.

So sudden was it, and so unexpected, that Buck was taken aback. He saw Spitz run out his scarlet tongue in a way he had of laughing; and he saw Francois, swinging an axe, spring into the mess of dogs. Three men with clubs were helping him to scatter them. It did not take long. Two minutes from the time Curly went down, the last of her assailants were clubbed off. But she lay there limp and lifeless in the bloody, trampled snow, almost literally torn to pieces, the swart half-breed standing over her and cursing horribly. The scene often came back to Buck to trouble him in his sleep. So that was the way. No fair play. Once down, that was the end of you. Well, he would see to it that he never went down. Spitz ran out his tongue and laughed again, and from that moment Buck hated him with a bitter and deathless hatred.

Before he had recovered from the shock caused by the tragic passing of Curly, he received another shock. Francois fastened upon him an arrangement of straps and buckles. It was a harness, such as he had seen the grooms put on the horses at home. And as he had seen horses work, so he was set to work, hauling Francois on a sled to the forest that fringed the valley, and returning with a load of firewood. Though his dignity was sorely hurt by thus being made a draught animal, he was too wise to rebel. He buckled down with a will and did his best, though it was all new and strange. Francois was stern, demanding instant obedience, and by virtue of his whip receiving instant obedience; while Dave, who was an experienced wheeler, nipped Buck's hindquarters whenever he was in error. Spitz was the leader, likewise experienced, and while he could not always get at Buck, he growled sharp reproof now and again, or cunningly threw his weight in the traces to jerk Buck into the way he should go. Buck learned easily, and under the combined tuition of his two mates and Francois made remarkable progress. Ere they returned to camp he knew enough to stop at "ho," to go ahead at "mush," to swing wide on the bends, and to keep clear of the wheeler when the loaded sled shot downhill at their heels.

So that was the way. No fair play. Once down, that was the end of you.

"Three very good dogs," Francois told Perrault. "Dat Buck, him pull like hell. I teach him quick as anything."

By afternoon, Perrault, who was in a hurry to be on the trail with his dispatches, returned with two more dogs. "Billee" and "Joe" he called them, two brothers, and true huskies both. Sons of the one mother though they were, they were different as day and night. Billee's one fault was his excessive good nature, while Joe was the very opposite, sour and introspective, with a perpetual snarl and a malignant eye. Buck received them in comradely fashion, Dave ignored them, while Spitz proceeded to thrash first one and then the other. Billee wagged his tail appeasingly, turned to run when he saw that appeasement was of no avail, and cried (still appeasingly) when Spitz's sharp teeth scored his flank. But no matter how Spitz circled, Joe whirled around on his heels to face him, mane bristling, ears laid back, lips writhing and snarling, jaws clipping together as fast as he could snap, and eyes diabolically gleaming—the incarnation of belligerent fear. So terrible was his appearance that Spitz was forced to forego disciplining him; but to cover his own discomfiture he turned upon the inoffensive and wailing Billee and drove him to the confines of the camp.

By evening Perrault secured another dog, an old husky, long and lean and gaunt, with a battle-scarred face and a single eye which flashed a warning of prowess that commanded respect. He was called Sol-leks, which means the Angry One. Like Dave, he asked nothing, gave nothing, expected nothing: and when he marched slowly and deliberately into their midst, even Spitz left him alone. He had one peculiarity which Buck was unlucky enough to discover. He did not like to be approached on his blind side. Of this offense Buck was unwittingly guilty, and the first knowledge he had of his indiscretion was when Sol-leks whirled upon him and slashed his shoulder to the bone for three inches up and down. Forever after Buck avoided his blind side, and to the last of their comradeship had no more trouble. His only apparent ambition, like Dave's, was to be left alone; though, as Buck was afterward to learn, each of them possessed one other and even more vital ambition.

That night Buck faced the great problem of sleeping. The tent, illumined by a candle, glowed warmly in the midst of the white plain; and when he, as a matter of course, entered it, both Perrault and Francois bombarded him with curses and cooking utensils, till he recovered from his consternation and fled ignominiously into the outer cold. A chill wind was blowing that nipped him sharply and bit with especial venom into his wounded shoulder. He lay down on the snow and attempted to sleep, but the frost soon drove him shivering to his feet. Miserable and disconsolate, he wandered about among the many tents, only to find that one place was as cold as another. Here and there savage dogs rushed upon him, but he bristled his neck-hair and snarled (for he was learning fast) and they let him go his way unmolested.

Finally an idea came to him. He would return and see how his own teammates were making out. To his astonishment, they had disappeared. Again he wandered about through the great camp, looking for them, and again he returned. Were they in the tent? No, that could not be, else he would not have been driven out. Then where could they possibly be? With drooping tail and shivering body, very forlorn indeed, he aimlessly circled the tent. Suddenly the snow gave way beneath his fore legs and he sank down. Something wriggled under his feet. He sprang back, bristling and snarling, fearful of the unseen and unknown. But a friendly little yelp reassured him, and he went back to investigate. A whiff of warm air ascended to his nostrils, and there, curled up under the snow in a snug ball, lay Billee. He whined placatingly, squirmed and wriggled to show his good will and intentions, and even ventured, as a bribe for peace, to lick Buck's face with his warm wet tongue.

Another lesson. So that was the way they did it, eh? Buck confidently selected a spot, and with much fuss and wasted effort proceeded to dig a hole for himself. In a trice the heat from his body filled the confined space and he was asleep. The day had been long and arduous, and he slept soundly and comfortably, though he growled and barked and wrestled with bad dreams.

Nor did he open his eyes till roused by the noises of the waking camp. At first he did not know where he was. It had snowed during the night and he was completely buried. The snow walls pressed him on every side, and a great surge of fear swept through him—the fear of the wild thing for the trap. It was a token that he was harking back through his own life to the lives of his forebears; for he was a civilized dog, an unduly civilized dog and of his own experience knew no trap and so could not of himself fear it. The muscles of his whole body contracted spasmodically and instinctively, the hair on his neck and shoulders stood on end, and with a ferocious snarl he bounded straight up into the blinding day, the snow flying about him in a flashing cloud. Ere he landed on his feet, he saw the white camp spread out before him and knew where he was and remembered all that had passed from the time he went for a stroll with Manuel to the hole he had dug for himself the night before.

A shout from Francois hailed his appearance. "What I say?" the dog-driver cried to Perrault. "Dat Buck for sure learn quick as anything."

Perrault nodded gravely. As courier for the Canadian Government, bearing important dispatches, he was anxious to secure the best dogs, and he was particularly gladdened by the possession of Buck.

Three more huskies were added to the team inside an hour, making a total of nine, and before another quarter of an hour had passed they were in harness and swinging up the trail toward the Yea Canyon. Buck was glad to be gone, and though the work was hard he found he did not particularly despise it. He was surprised at the eagerness which animated the whole team and which was communicated to him, but still more surprising was the change wrought in Dave and Sol-leks. They were new dogs, utterly transformed by the harness. All passiveness and unconcern had dropped from them. They were alert and active, anxious that the work should go well, and fiercely irritable with whatever, by delay or confusion, retarded that work. The toil of the traces seemed the supreme expression of their being, and all that they lived for and the only thing in which they took delight.

Dave was wheeler or sled dog, pulling in front of him was Buck, then came Sol-leks; the rest of the team was strung out ahead, single file, to the leader, which position was filled by Spitz. . . .

It was a hard day's run, up the Canyon, through Sheep Camp, past the Scales and the timber line, across glaciers and snowdrifts hundreds of feet deep, and over the great Chilcoot Divide, which stands between the salt water and the fresh and guards forbiddingly the sad and lonely North. They made good time down the chain of lakes which fills the craters of extinct volcanoes, and late that night pulled into the huge camp at the head of Lake Bennett, where thousands of gold-seekers were building boats against the breakup of the ice in the spring. Buck made his hole in the snow and slept the sleep of the exhausted just, but all too early was routed out in the cold darkness and harnessed with his mates to the sled.

That day they made forty miles, the trail being packed; but the next day, and for many days to follow, they broke their own trail, worked harder, and made poorer time. As a rule, Perrault traveled ahead of the team, packing the snow with webbed shoes to make it easier for them. Francois, guiding the sled at the gee-pole, sometimes exchanged places with him, but not often. Perrault was in a hurry, and he prided himself on his knowledge of ice, which knowledge was indispensable, for the fall ice was very thin, and where there was swift water, there was no ice at all.

Day after day, for days unending, Buck toiled in the traces. Always, they broke camp in the dark, and the first gray of dawn found them hitting the trail with fresh miles reeled off behind them. And always they pitched camp after dark, eating their bit of fish, and crawling to sleep into the snow. Buck was ravenous. The pound and a half of sundried salmon, which was his ration for each day, seemed to go nowhere. He never had enough, and suffered from perpetual hunger pangs. Yet the other dogs, because they weighed less and were born to the life, received a pound only of the fish and managed to keep in good condition.

He swiftly lost the fastidiousness which had characterized his old life. A dainty eater, he found that his mates, finishing first, robbed him of his unfinished ration. There was no defending it. While he was fighting off two or three, it was disappearing down the throats of the others. To remedy this, he ate as fast as they; and, so greatly did hunger compel him, he was not above taking what did not belong to him. He watched and learned. When he saw Pike, one of the new dogs, a clever malingerer and thief, slyly steal a slice of bacon when Perrault's back was turned, he duplicated the performance the following day, getting away with the whole chunk. A great uproar was raised, but he was unsuspected; while Dub, an awkward blunderer who was always getting caught, was punished for Buck's misdeed.

This first theft marked Buck as fit to survive in the hostile Northland environment. It marked his adaptability, his capacity to adjust himself to changing conditions, the lack of which would have meant swift and terrible death. It marked, further, the decay or going to pieces of his moral nature, a vain thing and a handicap in the ruthless struggle for existence. It was all well enough in the Southland, under the law of love and fellowship, to respect private property and personal feeling; but in the Northland, under the law of club and fang, whoso took such things into account was a fool, and in so far as he observed them he would fail to prosper.

Not that Buck reasoned it out. He was fit, that was all, and unconsciously he accommodated himself to the new mode of life. All his days, no matter what the odds, he had never run from a fight. But the club of the man in the red sweater had beaten into him a more fundamental and primitive code. Civilized, he could have died for a moral consideration, say the defense of Judge Miller's riding whip; but the completeness of his decivilization was now evidenced by his ability to flee from the defense of a moral consideration and so save his hide. He did not steal for the joy of it, but because of the clamor of his stomach. He did not rob openly, but stole secretly and cunningly, out of respect for club and fang. In short, the things he did were done because it was easier to do them than not to do them.

His development (or retrogression) was rapid. His muscles became hard as iron, and he grew callous to all ordinary pain. He achieved an internal as well as external economy. He could eat anything, no matter how loathsome or indigestible; and, once eaten, the juices of his stomach extracted the last least particle of nutriment; and his blood carried it to the farthest reaches of his body, building it into the toughest and stoutest of tissues. Sight and scent became remarkably keen, while his hearing developed such acuteness that in his sleep he heard the faintest sound and knew whether it heralded peace or peril. He learned to bite the ice out with his teeth when it collected between his toes; and when he was thirsty and there was a thick scum of ice over the water hole, he would break it by rearing and striking it with stiff fore legs. His most conspicuous trait was an ability to scent the wind and forecast it a night in advance. No matter how breathless the air when he dug his nest by tree or bank, the wind that later blew inevitably found him to leeward, sheltered and snug.

And not only did he learn by experience, but instincts long dead became alive again. The domesticated generations fell from him. In vague ways he remembered back to the youth of the breed, to the time the wild dogs ranged in packs through the primeval forest and killed their meat as they ran it down. It was no task for him to learn to fight with cut and slash and the quick wolf snap. In this manner had fought forgotten ancestors. They quickened the old life within him, and the old tricks which they had stamped into the heredity of the breed were his tricks. They came to him without effort or discovery, as though they had been his always. And when, on the still cold nights, he pointed his nose at a star and howled long and wolf-like, it was his ancestors, dead and dust, pointing nose at star and howling down through the centuries and through him. And his cadences were their cadences, the cadences which voiced their woe and what to them was the meaning of the stillness, and the cold, and dark.

Thus, as token of what a puppet thing life is, the ancient song surged through him and he came into his own again; and he came because men had found a yellow metal in the North, and because Manuel was a gardener's helper whose wages did not lap over the needs of his wife and divers small copies of himself.

Sources: The Jack London Online Collection (http://london.sonoma.edu); Jack London, *The Call of the Wild* (New York: The Macmillan Company, 1903).

Muckraking

The muckrakers were a group of journalists, novelists, and photographers who exposed the evils associated with industrialization, urbanization, and machine politics around the turn of the twentieth century. President Theodore Roosevelt coined the term in a speech in Washington, D.C., on April 14, 1906. Alluding to John Bunyan's Christian classic *Pilgrim's Progress* (1678), Roosevelt spoke of the character who, "with the Muck-rake [manure fork] in his hand," would rather rake filth than lift his eyes to nobler things. Said the president, "Men with the muck-rakes are often indispensable to the well-being of society; but only if they know when to stop raking the muck." While Roosevelt recognized that the modern-day muckrakers had helped build support for his own progressive reforms, he was concerned that their reporting was causing turmoil. In some cases, he believed that their allegations and rhetoric went too far; in other cases, he was suspicious of their leftist politics. For their part, the muckrakers shared a belief that they were working to advance American society. Looking back, there is little doubt that they played a key role in shaping public opinion and social policy at a critical time.

Although muckraking reached its peak in the first decade of the twentieth century, its origins can be traced to the rise of industrialization in the years following the Civil War. Massive economic transformation was causing widespread social disruption and glaring disparities between the lives of the rich and the poor. Advances in print technology and a drop in paper prices made it possible to publish inexpensive illustrated books and mass-circulation magazines. Rising literacy rates meant that more Americans were seeking reading material. By the turn of the century, all the elements were in place for investigative journalists to make their mark on American society.

Heralding the movement was a series of hard-hitting articles and original photographs in 1889 by Danish immigrant Jacob Riis that described the wretched living conditions in the slums of New York City for readers of the *Evening Sun*. A book-length version, *How the Other Half Lives*, appeared the following year and led to sweeping reform in state laws pertaining to tenement construction and the use of urban space.

Several widely circulating periodicals after the turn of the century, especially *McClure's Magazine*, became the primary vehicles for muckraking journalism—sometimes followed by book versions. Under the editorship of founder S.S. McClure, whose mission was to expose venality and corruption among the rich and powerful, *McClure's* alone published exposés on the oil industry by Ida Tarbell that would become *The History of the Standard Oil Company* (1904); on corruption in city and state politics by Lincoln Steffens that would become *The Shame of the Cities* (1904); on big steel ("What the U.S. Steel Corporation Really Is," 1901), coal mine conditions and labor racketeering ("The Right to Work," 1903), and racial violence ("What is a Lynching?," 1905) by Ray Stannard Baker; and scores of others.

In addition to *McClure's*, popular turn-of-the-century magazines that featured regular muckraking articles included *Collier's Weekly* (published by P.F. Collier), *Munsey's Magazine* (Frank Munsey), *Everybody's Magazine* (John Wanamaker), *Cosmopolitan* (John Brisben Walker), and *American Magazine* (formerly *Frank Leslie's*). The range of issues addressed by muckraking journalists was virtually unbounded, including stock and insurance manipulation (Thomas W. Lawson); business monopolies (Henry Demarest Lloyd); child labor (Edwin Markham, John Spargo, and photographer Lewis Hine); chronic unemployment (Frances Kellor); patent medicines (Samuel Hopkins Adams); the beef trust, the tobacco trust, and the church (Charles Edward Russell); and corruption in the U.S. Senate (David Graham Phillips).

Russell's early accounts of the Chicago stockyards for *Everybody's Magazine* were the inspiration for the most influential of all works of muckraking fiction, Upton Sinclair's *The Jungle* (1906). Other notable muckraking novels include Frank Norris's *The Octopus* (1901), about the railroad industry's invasion of the California wheat fields, and its sequel, *The Pit* (1903), on wheat speculation in the Chicago Board of Trade.

Muckraking in all its forms appealed to the emotions of middle-class readers and stressed that all Americans bore some responsibil-

McClure's Magazine

VOL. XX   *NOVEMBER, 1902*   NO. 1

THE HISTORY OF THE STANDARD OIL
COMPANY

BY IDA M. TARBELL

Author of "The Life of Lincoln"

CHAPTER I—THE BIRTH OF AN INDUSTRY

ONE of the busiest corners of the uct, petroleum, which had made this change
globe at the opening of the year from wilderness to market-place. This prod-
1872 was a strip of Northwestern uct in twelve years had not only peopled
Pennsylvania, not over fifty miles long, a waste place of the earth, it had revolu-
known the world over tionized the world's meth-
as the Oil Regions. ods of illumination and
Twelve years before, this added millions upon mil-
strip of land had been but lions of dollars to the
little better than a wil- wealth of the United
derness its only inhab- States.
itants the lumbermen, who Petroleum as a curiosity
every season cut great was no new thing. For
swaths of primeval pine more than two hundred
and hemlock from its years it had been de-
hills, and in the spring scribed in the journals
floated them down the of Western explorers. For
Allegheny River to Pitts- decades it had been dipped
burg. The great tides of up from the surface of
Western emigration had springs, soaked up by
shunned the spot for years blankets from running
as too rugged and un- streams, found in quan-
friendly for settlement, tities when salt wells were
and yet in twelve years bored, bottled and sold as
this region avoided by a cure-all—"Seneca Oil"
men had been transformed or "Rock Oil," it was
into a bustling trade cen- called. One man had even
ter, where towns elbowed distilled it in a crude way,
each other for place, into and sold it as an illu-
which the three great minant. Scientists had
trunk railroads had built described it, and travelers
branches, and every foot from the West often car-
of whose soil was fought ried bottles to their sci-
for by capitalists. It was entific friends in the
the discovery and devel- East. It was such a bot-
opment of a new raw prod- tleful, brought as a gift

GEORGE H. BISSELL

The man to whom more than any other is
due the credit of what is called the "discovery"
of oil; for it was he who first took steps to find its
value and to organize a company to produce it.
It was he, too, who suggested the means of getting oil which proved practical. After the oil
company which he organized obtained oil in the
Drake well, he aided in establishing the needed
industries and institutions in the new country.

Copyright, 1902, by the S. S. McClure Co. All rights reserved.

Ida M. Tarbell's muckraking classic, *The History of the Standard Oil Company*,
first appeared as a series of 19 articles in *McClure's Magazine*, beginning in
November 1902.

ity for the fraud, corruption, exploitation, inequality, and injustice in
American society. Much as Jacob Riis's reporting and photographs of
the tenements of New York City led to reforms at the state level, so the
work of muckrakers after the turn of the century proved instrumental
in achieving notable reforms at the federal level. Public outrage over
Upton Sinclair's graphic descriptions of Chicago meatpacking in
The Jungle led directly to passage of the Meat Inspection Act of 1906.
That work, along with Samuel Hopkins Adams's 11-article series for

Collier's Weekly in 1905, "The Great American Fraud," exerted pressure that resulted in the Pure Food and Drug Act of 1906. Lewis Hine's photographs hastened passage of the nation's first child-labor law, the Keating-Owen Act of 1916. And Tarbell's exposé of Standard Oil was instrumental in the breakup of that corporate giant by the U.S. Supreme Court in 1911 (*Standard Oil Co. of New Jersey v. United States*).

Muckraking fervor began to die down in the latter part of the decade, especially with U.S. entry into World War I. Legislation had addressed many of the strongest complaints, while other issues proved too complex and controversial for quick resolution. Yet the spirit of investigative journalism begun by the muckrakers lived on. Carriers of the muckraking tradition would come to include the likes of Rachel Carson, whose *Silent Spring* (1962) revealed the environmental ravages of pesticides; Edward R. Murrow, whose *Harvest of Shame* television documentary in 1960 exposed the plight of migrant farmworkers; Ralph Nader, whose *Unsafe at Any Speed* (1965) focused on the dangers of American automobiles; and all the print, television, and online investigative journalists who have shed light on fraud, corruption, and breaches of public trust in institutions of business and government.

Caryn E. Neumann and Jeff Hacker

See also: Naturalism; Riis, Jacob; Sinclair, Upton

◇◇

Chapter Ten, "Cutting to Kill," *The History of the Standard Oil Company*, Vol. 2 (excerpt), 1904

◇◇

Ida Minerva Tarbell's muckraking classic, The History of the Standard Oil Company, *first published as a series of articles in* McClure's Magazine, *exposed the ruthless competitive practices of that multinational industrial giant and the acquisitiveness of its founder, John D. Rockefeller. Tarbell, the daughter of a small Pennsylvania oil producer put out of business by Standard Oil, turned up damaging internal documents and interviewed a number of former employees and managers in what she called "a steady, painstaking work." Her exposé ultimately brought down Rockefeller and led to the breakup of the Standard Oil trust, as the U.S. Supreme Court ruled in*

1911 that the company was an illegal monopoly and should be divided into 34 smaller, independent firms. In Chapter Ten of the book, a landmark of both investigative reporting and corporate history, Tarbell describes Rockefeller's controlling approach to business and his efforts to organize global oil markets in much the same way as he had organized refining and transport.

To know every detail of the oil trade, to be able to reach at any moment its remotest point, to control even its weakest factor—this was John D. Rockefeller's ideal of doing business. It seemed to be an intellectual necessity for him to be able to direct the course of any particular gallon of oil from the moment it gushed from the earth until it went into the lamp of a housewife. There must be nothing—nothing in his great machine he did not know to be working right. It was to complete this ideal, to satisfy this necessity, that he undertook, late in the seventies, to organise the oil markets of the world, as he had already organised oil refining and oil transporting. Mr. Rockefeller was driven to this new task of organisation not only by his own curious intellect; he was driven to it by that thing so abhorrent to his mind—competition. If, as he claimed, the oil business belonged to him, and if, as he had announced, he was prepared to refine all the oil that men would consume, it followed as a corollary that the markets of the world belonged to him. In spite of his bold pretensions and his perfect organisation, a few obstinate oil refiners still lived and persisted in doing business. They were a fly in his ointment, a stick in his wonderful wheel. He must get them out; otherwise the Great Purpose would be unrealised. And so, while engaged in organising the world's markets, he incidentally carried on a campaign against those who dared intrude there.

When Mr. Rockefeller began to gather the oil markets into his hands he had a task whose field was literally the world, for already, in 1871, the year before he first appeared as an important factor in the oil trade, refined oil was going into every civilised country of the globe. Of the five and a half million barrels of crude oil produced that year, the world used five millions, over three and a half of which went to foreign lands. This was the market which had been built up in the first ten years of business by the men who had developed the oil territory and invented the processes of refining and transporting, and this was the market, still further developed, of course, that Mr. Rockefeller inherited when he succeeded in corralling the refining and transporting of oil. It was this market he proceeded to organise.

The process of organisation seems to have been natural and highly intelligent. The entire country was buying refined oil for illumination. Many refiners had their own agents out looking for markets; others sold to wholesale dealers, or jobbers, who placed trade with local dealers, usually grocers. Mr. Rockefeller's business was to replace independent agents and jobbers by his own employees. The United States was mapped out and agents appointed over these great divisions. Thus, a certain portion of the Southwest—including Kansas, Missouri, Arkansas and Texas—the Waters-Pierce Oil Company, of St. Louis, Missouri, had charge of; a portion of the South—including Kentucky, Tennessee and Mississippi—Chess, Carley and Company, of Louisville, Kentucky, had charge of. These companies in turn divided their territory into sections, and put the subdivisions in the charge of local agents. These local agents had stations where oil was received and stored, and from which they and their salesmen carried on their campaigns. This system, inaugurated in the seventies, has been developed until now the Standard Oil Company of each state has its own marketing department, whose territory is divided and watched over in the above fashion. The entire oil-buying territory of the country is thus covered by local agents reporting to division headquarters. These report in turn to the head of the state marketing department, and his reports go to the general marketing headquarters in New York. . . .

But the Standard Oil agents were not sent into a territory back in the seventies simply to sell all the oil they could by efficient service and aggressive pushing; they were sent there to sell all the oil that was bought. "The coal-oil business belongs to us," was Mr. Rockefeller's motto, and from the beginning of his campaign in the markets his agents accepted and acted on that principle. If a dealer bought but a barrel of oil a year, it must be from Mr. Rockefeller.

Sources: Internet Archive (http://archive.org); Ida M. Tarbell, *The History of the Standard Oil Company* (New York: McClure, Phillips, & Co., 1904).

Naturalism

Naturalism was a literary movement of the late nineteenth and early twentieth centuries that attempted to apply scientific principles of objectivity and detachment to the study of the human condition. Through the objective study of what the French novelist Émile Zola called "human beasts," naturalist writers believed they could discover and understand the natural laws that govern human lives without necessarily making moral judgments. They believed that human behavior is conditioned—even determined—by the combined forces of heredity and environment, over which the individual has little or no control, and that people are directed by their passions and instincts more than by reason.

Although naturalism was in many ways an outgrowth of the literary movement of realism, which preceded it chronologically, they differed in important ways. While the realists focused on the individual's struggle to maintain personal integrity in the face of an increasingly mechanistic and dehumanizing world, the naturalists concentrated more on the struggle for physical survival under those conditions. While the realists sought mainly to describe the world, the naturalists wanted to change it, even by revolutionary means if necessary. While the realists focused on middle- and upper-middle-class protagonists, the naturalists concentrated more on the lives of the lower-middle and working classes. Both dealt with the local, the commonplace, and the contemporary in everyday lives. But the naturalists were more inclined to endow ordinary people with the qualities of, or expect their actions to be those associated with, heroes and adventurers—violence and passion, the pursuit of sexual exploits, or feats of physical power resulting in desperate situations or brutal death.

Critic George Becker has defined naturalism as "pessimistic materialistic determinism." Literary historian Eric Sundquist has characterized naturalist writers as "reveling in the extraordinary, the excessive, and the grotesque in order to reveal the immutable bestiality of Man in Nature" and to dramatize "the loss of individuality at a psychological level by making a Calvinism without God its determining order and violent death as its utopia."

Inspired in part by Zola's *The Experimental Novel* (1880), Charles Darwin's scientific determinism, and Herbert Spencer's Social Darwinism (Darwin's principle of the survival of the fittest applied to human affairs), American naturalists viewed a person's circumstances, whether good or bad, primarily in terms of random, external, and biological forces. Specifically, they saw heredity and environment as playing disproportionate roles in influencing the disposition of their characters. Naturalistic writers—adopting a kind of literary scientific method—sought to interpret the natural laws behind these life-shaping forces as much as the actual behavior of the person under study. In many ways, their novels gave dramatic force to the revelations of such muckraking journalists as Ida Tarbell, Upton Sinclair, Jacob Riis, and Lincoln Steffens.

Among the leading practitioners of American naturalist literature were Stephen Crane (*Red Badge of Courage* and *Maggie: A Girl of the Streets*); Theodore Dreiser (*Sister Carrie, The Titan, The Financier,* and *An American Tragedy*); Jack London (*The Sea-Wolf* and *The Call of the Wild*); and Frank Norris (*McTeague, The Octopus,* and *The Pit*). Their influence also can be seen in the works of such later novelists as James T. Farrell, James Jones, John Steinbeck, Saul Bellow, and Nelson Algren.

Charles Pennacchio

See also: Anderson, Sherwood; Crane, Stephen; Dreiser, Theodore; London, Jack; Realism; Sinclair, Upton

Realism

Realism was a literary movement that came to the forefront in the United States during the late nineteenth century through the writings of William Dean Howells, Mark Twain, Henry James, and Kate Chopin, among others. Styling their work as a revolt against the "genteel tradition" of Romanticism and Transcendentalism, literary realists aimed at the faithful representation of contemporary social and personal reality, sought to portray people and things as they really are, and stressed perceptual experience as opposed to suggestive expression in metaphor or abstraction.

Strictly speaking a technique of writing, realism also focused on two overarching subjects and themes: the representation of middle- and upper-middle-class life and the conflict between the inherited American faith in individuals and humanity versus the pessimistic, deterministic creed of modern science. A direct reaction against the romantic idealism of the first half of the nineteenth century, works of literary realism embodied the period's growing faith in the scientific method, systematic study of history through documentary evidence, and increasing interest in rational philosophy.

Unlike naturalism, the literary movement that flowed out of it, literary realism did not engage in social criticism or seek to reform society. Above all, it aspired to accurate portrayal of life as it really is and the faithful depiction of the outside world based on objective observation. According to cultural historians William Harmon and C. Hugh Holman in their reference work *A Handbook to Literature* (1986), "Where romanticists transcend the immediate to find the ideal, and naturalists plumb the actual or superficial to find the scientific laws that control its actions, realists center their attention to a remarkable degree on the immediate, the here and now, the specific action, and the verifiable consequence."

The realist movement in Western literature began in mid-nine-teenth-century France with works by such novelists as Gustave Flaubert and Honoré de Balzac, was introduced to England by novelist George Eliot (Mary Ann Evans), and found a champion in the United States with the author and editor William Dean Howells. In addition to writing such realist novels as *The Rise of Silas Lapham* (1885), *A Hazard of New Fortunes* (1890), and *A Traveler from Altruria* (1894), Howells, as editor of *The Atlantic Monthly* and *Harper's New Monthly Magazine,* promoted efforts in realistic and local-color fiction by younger writers. Such works struck a responsive chord among Americans beset with rapid, massive, and often bewildering changes wrought by geographical expansion, industrialism, urbanization, immigration, and the growth of leisure and literacy among the ex-panding middle class. Realists focused, in regional and local terms, on the limiting effects of outside forces on human control and choice. Thus, in one view, realism was a kind of strategy for managing the threats of social change.

While their narrative backdrops varied, from Kate Chopin's treat-ment of women's roles and marriage to Upton Sinclair's stories of in-dustrial laborers, Paul Laurence Dunbar's tales of African American lives, and Mark Twain's Mississippi River adventures, each of these authors struck common themes. Among them were traditional (Old World or rural) values under siege, the struggle of urban and rural families to build and maintain a measure of domestic stability, capi-talism's ruthless exploitation of workers, and the practical struggles of a true-to-life protagonist against mounting social chaos. Works of literary realism thus captivated a society weaned on the promise of science as a force of salvation, eternally rational and progressive.

Charles Pennacchio

See also: Bierce, Ambrose; Chopin, Kate; Dunbar, Paul Laurence; Howells, William Dean; James, Henry; London, Jack; Naturalism; Twain, Mark

Riis, Jacob
(1849–1914)

A muckraking journalist, photographer, and social reformer, Jacob August Riis was a tireless advocate of decent housing for New York's lower classes and the author of one of the bibles of the municipal reform movement, *How the Other Half Lives* (1890).

The son of a schoolteacher and homemaker, Riis was born in Ribe, Denmark, on May 3, 1849. After apprenticing as a carpenter in Copenhagen but finding little work, he emigrated to the United States at age 21, traveling steerage in a steamship. He worked at various trades for three years in New York City before finding a job as a journalist with the *South Brooklyn News* in 1874. While gaining firsthand knowledge of the destitution and squalor in the city's slum areas, he landed a job as police reporter for the *New York Tribune* in 1877 and attempted to use the position as a platform for publicizing life in the tenements. Working the night beat on Manhattan's Lower East Side, he came to believe that "the poor were the victims rather than the makers of their fate"—a view he advanced in the strident, vivid, sometimes melodramatic prose style he developed.

Riis moved on to a position as photojournalist for the New York *Evening Sun* in 1888. As one of the first professional photographers to use flash powder, he exposed the wretched living and working conditions in the recesses of overcrowded immigrant districts such as the Five Points and Fourth Ward. Nineteen of Riis's photographs accompanied his article on tenement life in the December 1889 issue of *Scribner's Magazine;* his book-length version, *How the Other Half Lives,* appeared the following year. Combining his stark visual record with graphic text descriptions and a powerful indictment of the wealthy and powerful for allowing such conditions to develop, Riis sought to spread awareness of the problem and to lobby for rehabilitation. Of the notorious Mulberry Bend neighborhood he

Hard-hitting articles and stark photographs by Jacob Riis—including "Bandits' Roost" (1888)—shed light on the dismal living standards in New York City's tenements during the late 1800s.

wrote, "The whole district is a maze of narrow, often unsuspected passage ways—necessarily, for there is scarce a lot that has not two, three, or four tenements upon it, swarming with unwholesome crowds."

Theodore Roosevelt, who as president in 1906 would coin the term "muckraker," was among those whose attention Riis captured early on. When Roosevelt became police commissioner of New York City in 1895, he would accompany Riis on all-night tours of city neighborhoods to learn about street life and police work. In a tribute he wrote as president, Roosevelt called his old friend "the most useful citizen of New York."

Riis continued to write and lecture on the problems faced by the urban poor, spreading interest in social reform and setting a trend for future muckrakers. Subsequent books included *The Children of the Poor* (1892), *Out of Mulberry Street* (1898), *Children of the Tenements* (1903), and *Neighbors: Life Stories of the Other Half* (1914), as well as an autobiography, *The Making of an American* (1901).

Although Jacob Riis held only one official position, secretary of the New York City Small Parks Commission in 1897, his efforts brought sweeping improvements to the quality of urban life. New state laws mandated improvements in tenement construction, schools and playgrounds were built in slum areas, and the state's water system underwent a major renovation as a result of Riis's August 1891 exposé in the *Evening Sun* on the threat of cholera.

Riis died at his home in Barre, Massachusetts, on May 26, 1914. The Jacob Riis Houses on Manhattan's Lower East Side, a 13-building public housing complex completed in 1949, commemorates his work to improve living conditions for the urban poor.

Jennifer Harrison

See also: Muckraking

◇◇◇

Chapters One and Two, *How the Other Half Lives* (excerpts), 1890

◇◇◇

Like hundreds of thousands of other European immigrants in the mid- to late nineteenth century, Danish-born Jacob Riis lived in the poverty and squalor of the tenement houses on New York's Lower East Side. Raising urban living standards thus became his life's mission, which he pursued with pen and camera in a steady succession of magazine articles and books. The most influential was How the Other Half Lives, *from which the first two chapters are excerpted below. In tones alternately indignant, accusatory, and sympathetic, Riis calls attention to the spread of New York tenement life in all its destitution, overcrowding, disease, and sheer filth.*

I. Genesis of the Tenement

The first tenement New York knew bore the mark of Cain from its birth, though a generation passed before the waiting was deciphered. It was the "rear house," infamous ever after in our city's history. There had been tenant-houses before, but they were not built for the purpose. Nothing would probably have shocked their original owners more than the idea of their harboring a promiscuous crowd; for they were the decorous homes of the old Knickerbockers, the proud aristocracy of Manhattan in the early days.

It was the stir and bustle of trade, together with the tremendous immigration that followed upon the war of 1812 that dislodged them. In thirty-five years the city of less than a hundred thousand came to harbor half a million souls, for whom homes had to be found. . . . As business increased, and the city grew with rapid strides, the necessities of the poor became the opportunity of their wealthier neighbors, and the stamp was set upon the old houses, suddenly become valuable, which the best thought and effort of a later age has vainly struggled to efface. Their "*large* rooms were partitioned into *several smaller ones,* without regard to light or ventilation, the rate of rent being lower in proportion to space or height from the street; and they soon became filled from cellar to garret with a class of tenantry living from hand to mouth, loose in morals, improvident in habits, degraded, and squalid as beggary itself." It was thus the dark bedroom, prolific of untold depravities, came into the world. It was destined to survive the old houses. In their new role, says the old report, eloquent in its indignant denunciation of "evils more destructive than wars," "they were not intended to last. Rents were fixed high enough to cover damage and abuse from this class, from whom nothing was expected, and the most was made of them while they lasted. Neatness, order, cleanliness, were never dreamed of in connection with the tenant-house system, as it spread its localities from year to year; while redress slovenliness, discontent, privation, and ignorance were left to work out their invariable results, until the entire premises reached the level of tenant-house dilapidation, containing, but sheltering not, the miserable hordes that crowded beneath smouldering, water-rotted roofs or burrowed among the rats of clammy cellars." Yet so illogical is human greed that, at a later day, when called to account, "the proprietors frequently urged the filthy habits of the tenants as an excuse for the condition of their property, utterly losing sight of the fact that it was the tolerance of those habits which was the real evil, and that for this they themselves were alone responsible."

Still the pressure of the crowds did not abate, and in the old garden where the stolid Dutch burgher grew his tulips or early cabbages a rear house was built, generally of wood, two stories high at first. Presently it was carried lop another story, and another. Where two families had lived ten moved in. The front house followed suit, if the brick walls were strong enough. The question was not always asked, judging from complaints made by a contemporary witness, that the old buildings were "often carried up to a great height without regard to the strength of the foundation walls." It was rent the owner was after; nothing was said in the contract about either the safety or the comfort of the tenants. The garden gate no longer swung on its rusty hinges. The shell-paved walk had become an alley; what the rear house had left of the garden, a "court" Plenty such are yet to be found in the Fourth Ward, with here and there one of the original rear tenements.

Worse was to follow. It was "soon perceived by estate owners and agents of property that a greater percentage of profits could be realized by the conversion of houses and blocks into barracks, and dividing their space into smaller proportions capable of containing human life within four walls. . . . Blocks were rented of real estate owners, or 'purchased on time,' or taken in charge at a percentage, and held for under-letting." With the appearance of the middleman, wholly irresponsible, and utterly reckless and unrestrained, began the era of tenement building which turned out such blocks as Gotham Court, where, in one cholera epidemic that scarcely touched the clean wards, the tenants died at the rate of one hundred and ninety-five to the thousand of population; which forced the general mortality of the city up front 1 in 41.83 in 1815, to 1 in 27.33 in 1855. . . . The tenement-house population had swelled to half a million souls by that time, and on the East Side, in what is still the most densely populated district in all the world, China not excluded, it was packed at the rate of 290,000 to the square mile, a state of affairs wholly unexampled. The utmost cupidity of other lands and other days had never contrived to herd much more than half that number within the same space. The greatest crowding of Old London was at the rate of 175,816. Swine roamed the streets and gutters as their principal scavengers. The death of a child in a tenement was registered at the Bureau of Vital Statistics as "plainly due to suffocation in the foul air of an unventilated apartment," and the Senators, who had come down from Albany to find out what was the matter with New York, reported that "there are annually cut off from the population by disease and death enough human beings to people a city, and enough human labor to sustain it." And yet experts had testified that, as compared with uptown, rents were from twenty-five to thirty per cent and higher in the worst slums of the lower wards, with such accommodations as were enjoyed, for instance, by a "family with boarders" in Cedar Street, who fed hogs in the Stellar that contained eight or ten loads of manure; or "one room 12 x 19 with five families living in it, comprising twenty persons of both sexes and all ages, with only two beds, without partition, screen, chair, or table." The rate of rent has been successfully maintained to the present day, though the hog at least has been eliminated. . . .

II. Awakening

. . .

To-day, what is a tenement? The law defines it as a house "occupied by three or more families, living independently and doing their cooking on the premises; or by more than two families on a door, so living and cooking and having a common right in the halls, stairways, yards, etc." That is the legal meaning, and includes flats and apartment-houses, with which we have nothing to do. In its narrower sense the typical tenement was thus described when last arraigned before the bar of public justice: "It is generally a brick building from four to six stories high on the street, frequently with a store on the first floor which, when used for the sale of liquor, has a side opening for the benefit of the inmates and to evade the Sunday law; four families occupy each floor, and a set of rooms consists of one or two dark closets, used as bedrooms, with a living room twelve feet by ten. The staircase is too often a dark well in the centre of the house, and no direct through ventilation is possible, each family being separated from the other by partitions. Frequently the rear of the lot is occupied by another building of three stories high with two families on a floor." The picture is nearly as true to-day as ten years ago, and will be for a long time to come. The dim light admitted by the air-shaft shines upon greater crowds than ever. Tenements are still "good property," and the poverty of the poor man his destruction. A barrack down town where he *has to live* because he is poor brings in a third more rent than a decent flat house in Harlem. The statement once made a sensation that between seventy and eighty children had been found in one tenement. It no longer excites even passing atten-tion, when the sanitary police report counting 101 adults and 91 children in a Crosby Street house, one of twins, built together. The children in the other, if I am not mistaken, numbered 89, a total of 180 for two tenements! Or when a midnight inspec-tion in Mulberry Street unearths a hundred and fifty "lodgers" sleeping on filthy floors in two buildings. Spite of brown-stone trimmings, plate-glass and mosaic vestibule floors, the water does not rise in summer to the second story, while the beer flows unchecked to the all-night picnics on the roof. The sa-loon with the side-door and the landlord divide the prosperity of the place between them, and the tenant, in sullen submission, foots the bills.

> *The dim light admitted by the air-shaft shines upon greater crowds than ever.*

Where are the tenements of to-day? Say rather: where are they not? In fifty years they have crept up from the Fourth Ward slums and the Five Points the whole length of the island, and have polluted the Annexed District to the Westchester line. Crowding all the lower wards, wherever business leaves a foot of ground unclaimed; strung along both rivers, like ball and chain tied to the foot of every street, and filling up Harlem with their rest-less, pent-up multitudes, they hold within their clutch the wealth and business of New York, hold them at their mercy in the day of mob-rule and wrath. The bullet-proof shutters, the stacks of hand-grenades, and the Gatling guns of the Sub-Treasury are tacit admissions of the fact and of the quality of the mercy expected.

The tenements to-day are New York, harboring three-fourths of its population. When another generation shall have doubled the census of our city, and to that vast army of workers, held captive by poverty, the very name of home shall be as a bitter mockery, what will the harvest be?

Source: Jacob Riis, *How the Other Half Lives: Studies Among the Tenements of New York* (New York: Charles Scribner's Sons, 1890).

Robinson, Edwin Arlington

(1869–1935)

Regarded as America's most accomplished and influential poet of the early twentieth century, Edward Arlington Robinson brought a modernist colloquial voice, keen psychological insight, and uncommon technical mastery to his verse. He lived much of his early life in poverty and alcoholism, which greatly affected the subject matter of his early poems. Many dealt with the seeming failure and tragedy of individuals in the face of a repressive Puritan ethic and the crushing burdens of industrialism and materialism. Yet Robinson also asserted that public failure can be counterbalanced by one's life-affirming belief in a higher power. His "Tilbury Town cycle"—early collections named after the fictional New England town in which the poems are set—continues to occupy an esteemed place in American verse; his later work won three Pulitzer Prizes (1922, 1925, 1928).

Born in Head Tide, Maine, on December 22, 1869, Robinson was the third son of Edward and Mary Elizabeth (Palmer) Robinson. The family moved to Gardiner, Maine, a small town in the southeastern part of the state where his father was a successful timber merchant; Gardiner later served as the model for Tilbury Town. Robinson manifested a love for poetry and the literary classics at an early age. He attended Harvard University from 1891 to 1893 but was forced to drop out for family and financial reasons.

Returning to Gardiner, he wrote poems that were published in two collections—*The Torrent and the Night Before* (1896) and *The Children of the Night* (1897)—underwritten by friends. In 1900, Robinson moved to New York City, where he supported himself with temporary jobs while continuing to write poetry. Two years later, friends subsidized his next publication as well, *Captain Craig: A Book of Poems*.

Robinson's work remained largely ignored—and the poet increasingly dissolute—until 1905, when Kermit Roosevelt brought *The*

Children of the Night to the attention of his father, President Theodore Roosevelt. The president loved the book, wrote a laudatory review in *Outlook* magazine—"there is an undoubted touch of genius in the poems," he averred—and secured Robinson a position at the New York Customs House. This provided the poet with a steady income and allowed him to continue writing, at least while TR remained in the White House. When Roosevelt left the presidency in 1909, Robinson resigned from the customshouse and returned to Gardiner. His next collection in the Tilbury Town cycle, *The Town Down the River* (1910), was dedicated to the former president.

Moving to New York City after the dissolution of the family estate, Robinson began spending his summers at the MacDowell Colony in Peterborough, New Hampshire, a 200-acre farm founded by the widow of composer Edward MacDowell to provide a creative refuge for composers, artists, and writers. At Peterborough, Robinson both experimented with new literary forms, writing two plays, and expanded his poetic vision. His reputation grew. *The Man Against the Sky* (1916) won greater critical acclaim than any of his previous collections, and *Merlin* (1917), a long narrative poem based on the legend of King Arthur, forged fertile new ground that he would tap again in *Lancelot* (1920) and *Tristram* (1927), both highly successful.

Robinson's three Pulitzers came in 1922 (the first ever awarded in poetry) for his *Collected Poems* (1921), which also gave him financial independence for the first time in his life; in 1925 for *The Man Who Died Twice* (1924), a long psychological narrative about a street musician who descends into drunkenness and loses his masterpiece; and in 1928 for *Tristram*. Late works include *Amaranth* (1934) and *King Jasper* (1935), which he worked on up to his death.

Edwin Arlington Robinson, who had never married and lived most of his life in solitude, fell ill with cancer in early 1935 and died in New York City on April 6. In the introduction to *King Jasper,* published posthumously, fellow poet and New Englander Robert Frost wrote of Robinson's skill with traditional, rhymed verse while investing it with modernist energy and insights into the inner recesses of common human experience. "Robinson stayed content with the old-fashioned ways to be new," wrote Frost.

Harold D. Langley

See also: Naturalism; Realism

Selected Poems, 1897–1921

In his early verse, for which he is best known, Edwin Arlington Robinson earned a reputation as America's "poet laureate of unhappiness." His dark portrayals of ordinary men and women suffering life's ordeals, struggling to master their fate, have been described as stories of the American Dream gone awry. "Richard Cory," which first appeared in the collection The Children of the Night *(1897), distills the life of a wealthy and respected man about town—and his descent to suicide—in 16 lines. "Miniver Cheevy," from* The Town Down the River *(1910), is recognized as a mocking self-portrait of the poet as a romantic idealist. And "Mr. Flood's Party," which appeared in* Avon's Harvest *(1921), is another character sketch in verse but more modern in its wealth of symbolism and complexity of theme—time passing.*

"Richard Cory," 1897

Whenever Richard Cory went down town,
The people on the pavement looked at him:
He was a gentleman from sole to crown,
Clean favored, and imperially slim.

And he was always quietly arrayed,
And he was always human when he talked;
But still he fluttered pulses when he said,
"Good-morning," and he glittered when he walked.

And he was rich—yes, richer than a king—
And admirably schooled in every grace.
In fine, we thought that he was everything
To make us wish that we were in his place.

So on we worked, and waited for the light,
And went without the meat, and cursed the bread;
And Richard Cory, one calm summer night,
Went home and put a bullet through his head.

"Miniver Cheevy," 1910

Miniver Cheevy, child of scorn,
  Grew lean while he assailed the seasons;
He wept that he was ever born,
  And he had reasons.

Miniver loved the days of old
  When swords were bright and steeds were prancing;
The vision of a warrior bold
  Would set him dancing.

Miniver sighed for what was not,
  And dreamed, and rested from his labors;
He dreamed of Thebes and Camelot,
  And Priam's neighbors.

Miniver mourned the ripe renown
  That made so many a name so fragrant;
He mourned Romance, now on the town,
  And Art, a vagrant.

Miniver loved the Medici,
  Albeit he had never seen one;
He would have sinned incessantly
  Could he have been one.

Miniver cursed the commonplace
  And eyed a khaki suit with loathing;
He missed the mediæval grace
  Of iron clothing.

Miniver scorned the gold he sought,
  But sore annoyed was he without it;
Miniver thought, and thought, and thought,
  And thought about it.

Miniver Cheevy, born too late,
   Scratched his head and kept on thinking;
Miniver coughed, and called it fate,
   And kept on drinking.

"Mr. Flood's Party," 1921

Old Eben Flood, climbing alone one night
Over the hill between the town below
And the forsaken upland hermitage
That held as much as he should ever know
On earth again of home, paused warily.
The road was his with not a native near;
And Eben, having leisure, said aloud,
For no man else in Tilbury Town to hear:

"Well, Mr. Flood, we have the harvest moon
Again, and we may not have many more;
The bird is on the wing, the poet says,
And you and I have said it here before.
Drink to the bird." He raised up to the light
The jug that he had gone so far to fill,
And answered huskily: "Well, Mr. Flood,
Since you propose it, I believe I will."

Alone, as if enduring to the end
A valiant armor of scarred hopes outworn,
He stood there in the middle of the road
Like Roland's ghost winding a silent horn.
Below him, in the town among the trees,
Where friends of other days had honored him,
A phantom salutation of the dead
Rang thinly till old Eben's eyes were dim.

Then, as a mother lays her sleeping child
Down tenderly, fearing it may awake,
He set the jug down slowly at his feet

With trembling care, knowing that most things break;
And only when assured that on firm earth
It stood, as the uncertain lives of men
Assuredly did not, he paced away,
And with his hand extended paused again:

"Well, Mr. Flood, we have not met like this
In a long time; and many a change has come
To both of us, I fear, since last it was
We had a drop together. Welcome home!"
Convivially returning with himself,
Again he raised the jug up to the light;
And with an acquiescent quaver said:
"Well, Mr. Flood, if you insist, I might.

"Only a very little, Mr. Flood—
For auld lang syne. No more, sir; that will do."
So, for the time, apparently it did,
And Eben evidently thought so too;
For soon amid the silver loneliness
Of night he lifted up his voice and sang,
Secure, with only two moons listening,
Until the whole harmonious landscape rang—

"For auld lang syne." The weary throat gave out,
The last word wavered; and the song being done,
He raised again the jug regretfully
And shook his head, and was again alone.
There was not much that was ahead of him,
And there was nothing in the town below—
Where strangers would have shut the many doors
That many friends had opened long ago.

Sources: Poetry Foundation (www.poetryfoundation.org); Edward Arlington Robinson, *Collected Poems* (New York: Macmillan, 1921).

Sinclair, Upton
(1878–1968)

Known for his lifelong crusade on behalf of progressive reform, the novelist, journalist, social critic, and politician Upton Sinclair was a firm believer in the power of literature to improve the human condition. As one of the preeminent "muckraking" writers of his generation, he employed both fiction and nonfiction to expose official corruption, social injustice, and the need for reform wherever he found them. An untiring polemicist, he produced more than 90 novels, dozens of plays, 20 works of nonfiction, and an unending stream of articles, stories, and political tracts. By far his most celebrated work is *The Jungle* (1906), a powerful naturalistic novel that exposed wretched sanitary and working conditions in the Chicago meatpacking industry and that led to passage of the Pure Food and Drug Act and Meat Inspection Act later that year. With the exception of Harriet Beecher Stowe, author of *Uncle Tom's Cabin* (1852), no other novelist has had a greater impact on U.S. political history.

Upton Beall Sinclair, Jr., was born in Baltimore, Maryland, on September 20, 1878, and moved with his family to New York City at age 8. The son of an alcoholic father and puritanical mother, he was raised in poverty but spent long periods of time living with wealthy grandparents. Sinclair attended City College of New York, where he completed undergraduate studies in 1897, and did graduate work at Columbia University, where he supported himself by writing pulp fiction. He began his career as a novelist soon after leaving Columbia in 1901.

After joining the Socialist Party and marrying in 1902, Sinclair produced several conventional romance and adventure novels that sold poorly. In 1904, working undercover for the socialist newspaper *Appeal to Reason,* he spent seven weeks experiencing conditions in the stockyards of Chicago. His report, in fictional form, was serialized in

Upton Sinclair's muckraking novel *The Jungle* (1906) revealed the unsanitary conditions and labor abuses in Chicago's meatpacking industry, leading directly to Progressive Era reforms.

the paper during the summer of 1905 and appeared as a book-length novel, *The Jungle,* the following February.

The book was a national sensation, selling more than 150,000 copies in the first months; it went on to be published in 17 languages. While Sinclair had hoped that his account would arouse sympathy for stockyard workers, public indignation instead focused on food safety and the deplorable sanitary conditions in the industry. Sinclair was quoted as saying, "I aimed at the public's heart and by accident I hit it in the stomach." President Theodore Roosevelt, who found Sinclair's socialist views abhorrent, nevertheless read the book and called for a federal investigation of the meatpacking industry. The White House released the report to Congress in early June, and public pressure helped gain passage of the two major reform bills that Roosevelt signed into law before the end of the month.

The Jungle also gave impetus to the brand of investigative journalism that President Roosevelt pejoratively dubbed "muckraking." Social justice and reform would remain the major themes of Sinclair's own work for the next five decades. The novels *King Coal* (1917), *Oil!* (1927), and *Little Steel* (1938) explored the lives of workers in large energy corporations, exposing corruption and greed in much the same way *The Jungle* had. Institutions in religion, journalism, education, and the arts faced similar scrutiny in, respectively, *The Profits of Religion* (1918), *The Brass Check* (1919), *The Goslings* (1924), and *Mammonart* (1925); *Boston* (1928) was a "documentary novel" about the Sacco and Vanzetti murder case and an indictment of the criminal justice system.

Sinclair's other works include 11 historical novels known as the Lanny Budd series, which together comprise a loose fictional history of the United States and Europe between the two world wars. The first book in the series, *World's End* (1940), examines the life of an antifascist hero. *Dragon's Teeth* (1942), about Adolf Hitler's rise to power in Nazi Germany, won the 1943 Pulitzer Prize for Fiction. And the final novel in the series, *The Return of Lanny Budd* (1953), explores U.S. hostility toward post–World War II Soviet Russia.

For Sinclair personally, proceeds from the sale of *The Jungle* provided the funds to open an experimental cooperative-living community called Helicon Home Colony in Englewood, New Jersey, a utopian-socialist project that lasted until fire destroyed the facility in 1907. Sinclair was married three times (his second marriage lasted more than 48 years). He moved to California in the 1920s and lived there for more than four decades. He founded a forerunner of the League for Industrial Democracy and the Southern California branch of the American Civil Liberties Union. During the Great Depression of the 1930s, he organized a socialist reform movement called End Poverty in California (EPIC). In the most successful of several forays into electoral politics, he mounted a major campaign for governor of California in 1934, as a Democrat on the EPIC platform; despite heavy media coverage, he lost to Republican Frank Merriam by a sizable margin.

Sinclair continued to write and campaign for social justice until his final years. He died at the age of 90 in Bound Brook, New Jersey, on November 25, 1968.

Rod Phillips and Yuwu Song

See also: Crane, Stephen; Dreiser, Theodore; Muckraking; Naturalism

Chapter Nine, *The Jungle* (excerpt), 1906

The protagonist of Upton Sinclair's historic muckraking novel The Jungle *is a Lithuanian immigrant named Jurgis Rudkus, who believes that hard work will allow him to prosper in America despite the miserable conditions in the Chicago meatpacking plant where he is employed. Ultimately, Rudkus becomes disillusioned by the squalor, disease, and life of poverty the workers must endure and turns to socialism as a way of fighting company oppression. The excerpt that follows contains the kind of behind-the-scene descriptions that shocked readers everywhere and galvanized public demand for America's first major food safety legislation.*

Jurgis heard of these things little by little, in the gossip of those who were obliged to perpetrate them. It seemed as if every time you met a person from a new department, you heard of new swindles and new crimes. There was, for instance, a Lithuanian who was a cattle butcher for the plant where Marija had worked, which killed meat for canning only; and to hear this man describe the animals which came to his place would have been worth while for a Dante or a Zola. It seemed that they must have agencies all over the country, to hunt out old and crippled and diseased cattle to be canned. There were cattle which had been fed on "whiskey-malt," the refuse of the breweries, and had become what the men called "steerly"—which means covered with boils. It was a nasty job killing these, for when you plunged your knife into them they would burst and splash foul-smelling stuff into your face; and when a man's sleeves were smeared with blood, and his hands steeped in it, how was he ever to wipe his face, or to clear his eyes so that he could see? It was stuff such as this that made the "embalmed beef" that had killed several times as many United States soldiers as all the bullets of the Spaniards; only the army beef, besides, was not fresh canned, it was old stuff that had been lying for years in the cellars.

Men welcomed tuberculosis in the cattle they were feeding, because it made them fatten more quickly. . . .

Then one Sunday evening, Jurgis sat puffing his pipe by the kitchen stove, and talking with an old fellow whom Jonas had introduced, and who worked in the canning-rooms at Durham's; and so Jurgis learned a few things about the great and only Durham canned goods, which had become a national institution. They were regular alchemists at Durham's; they advertised a mushroom-catsup, and the men who made it did not know what a mushroom looked like. They advertised "potted chicken,"— and it was like the boarding-house soup of the comic papers, through which a chicken had walked with rubbers on. Perhaps they had a secret process for making chickens chemically—who knows? said Jurgis's friend; the things that went into the mixture were tripe, and the fat of pork, and beef suet, and hearts of beef, and finally the waste ends of veal, when they had any. They put these up in several grades, and sold them at several prices; but the contents of the cans all came out of the same hopper. And then there was "potted game" and "potted grouse," "potted ham," and "devilled ham"—de-vyled, as the men called it. "De-vyled" ham was made out of the waste ends of smoked beef that were too small to be sliced by the machines; and also tripe, dyed with chemicals so that it would not show white; and trimmings of hams and corned beef; and potatoes, skins and all; and finally the hard cartilaginous gullets of beef, after the tongues had been cut out. All this ingenious mixture was ground up and flavored with spices to make it taste like something. Anybody who could invent a new imitation had been sure of a fortune from old Durham, said Jurgis's informant; but it was hard to think of anything new in a place where so many sharp wits had been at work for so long;

where men welcomed tuberculosis in the cattle they were feeding, because it made them fatten more quickly; and where they bought up all the old rancid butter left over in the grocery-stores of a continent, and "oxidized" it by a forced-air process, to take away the odor, rechurned it with skim milk, and sold it in bricks in the cities! Up to a year or two ago it had been the custom to kill horses in the yards—ostensibly for fertilizer; but after long agitation the newspapers had been able to make the public realize that the horses were being canned. Now it was against the law to kill horses in Packingtown, and the law was really complied with—for the present, at any rate. Any day, however, one might see sharp-horned and shaggy-haired creatures running with the sheep—and yet what a job you would have to get the public to believe that a good part of what it buys for lamb and mutton is really goat's flesh!

There was another interesting set of statistics that a person might have gathered in Packingtown—those of the various afflictions of the workers. When Jurgis had first inspected the packing-plants with Szedvilas, he had marvelled while he listened to the tale of all the things that were made out of the carcasses of animals, and of all the lesser industries that were maintained there; now he found that each one of these lesser industries was a separate little inferno, in its way as horrible as the killing-beds, the source and fountain of them all. The workers in each of them had their own peculiar diseases. And the wandering visitor might be sceptical about all the swindles, but he could not be sceptical about these, for the worker bore the evidence of them about on his own person—generally he had only to hold out his hand.

There were the men in the pickle-rooms, for instance, where old Antanas had gotten his death; scarce a one of these that had not some spot of horror on his person. Let a man so much as scrape his finger pushing a truck in the pickle-rooms, and he might have a sore that would put him out of the world; all the joints in his fingers might be eaten by the acid, one by one. Of the butchers and floorsmen, the beef-boners and trimmers, and all those who used knives, you could scarcely find a person who had the use of his thumb; time and time again the base of it had been slashed, till it was a mere lump of flesh against which the man pressed the knife to hold it. The hands of these men would be criss-crossed with cuts, until you could no longer pretend to count them or to trace them. They would have no nails,—they had worn them off pulling hides; their knuckles were swollen so that their fingers spread out like a fan. There were men who worked in the cooking-rooms, in the midst of steam and sickening odors, by artificial light; in these rooms the germs of tuberculosis might live for two years, but the supply was renewed every hour. There were the beef-luggers, who carried two-hundred-pound quarters into the refrigerator-cars; a fearful kind of work, that began at four o'clock in the morning, and that wore out the most powerful men in a few years. There were those who worked in the chilling-rooms, and whose special disease was rheumatism; the time-limit that a man could work in the chilling-rooms was said to be five years. There were the woolpluckers, whose hands went to pieces even sooner than the hands of the pickle-men; for the pelts of the sheep had to be painted with acid to loosen the wool, and then the pluckers had to pull out this wool with their bare hands, till the acid had eaten their fingers off. There were those who made the tins for the canned-meat; and their hands, too, were a maze of cuts, and each cut represented a chance for blood-poisoning. Some worked at the stamping-machines, and it was very seldom that one could work long there at the pace that was set, and not give out and forget himself, and have a part of his hand chopped off. There were the "hoisters," as they were called, whose task it was to press the lever which lifted the dead cattle off the floor. They ran along upon a rafter, peering down through the damp and the steam; and as old Durham's architects had not built the killing-room for the convenience of the hoisters, at every few feet they would have to stoop under a beam, say four feet above the one they ran on; which got them into the habit of stooping, so that in a few years they would be walking like chimpanzees. Worst of any, however, were the fertilizer-men, and those who served in the cooking-rooms. These people could not be shown to the visitor,—for the odor of a fertilizer-man would scare any ordinary visitor at a hundred yards, and as for the other men, who worked in tank-rooms full of steam, and in some of which there were open vats near the level of the floor, their peculiar trouble was that they fell into the vats; and when they were fished out, there was never enough of them left to be worth exhibiting,—sometimes they would be overlooked for days, till all but the bones of them had gone out to the world as Durham's Pure Leaf Lard!

Sources: Project Gutenberg (www.gutenberg.org); Upton Sinclair, *The Jungle* (New York: Doubleday, Page & Company, 1906).

Turner, Frederick Jackson
(1861–1932)

Although he wrote relatively few books and papers, historian Frederick Jackson Turner contributed ideas that radically altered the study and writing of American history and that are still debated among academics today. His 1893 paper "The Significance of the Frontier in American History" articulated what became known as the "frontier thesis," or "Turner thesis," which explained the importance of America's pioneering past to the formation of national character and institutions.

Turner was born on November 14, 1861, in Portage, Wisconsin, where he attended public schools. His father, a journalist and amateur local historian, piqued his interest in the study of the past. Turner received a bachelor's degree in 1884 from the University of Wisconsin, where he studied under classical scholar William Francis Allan and was exposed to the then novel idea of evolving societies. Turner earned his doctorate in history from Johns Hopkins University in 1890, with a dissertation on the Native American fur trade in Wisconsin. He returned to the University of Wisconsin as a history professor in 1890 and taught there for 20 years. He moved to Harvard University in 1910 and remained there until retiring in 1924.

Turner delivered his groundbreaking paper on the frontier at a meeting of the American Historical Association held on July 12, 1893, at the World's Columbian Exposition in Chicago. Turner's thesis was prompted by the 1890 report of the Bureau of the Census, according to which a distinctive American frontier had disappeared with the spread of the population into the open spaces of the West. This "closing of the American frontier," in Turner's view, marked the end of 300 years of expansion that recapitulated the development of the nation's character from generation to generation. Countering the prevailing view that European origins and influences had shaped the nation's development, Turner argued that the Western frontier—"the existence of an area of free land, its continuous recession, and the advance of American settlement"—played a defining role in the establishment of American democracy and the nation's core values of optimism, pragmatism, individualism, mobility, and materialism. Contemporary historians and political leaders such as Theodore Roosevelt welcomed Turner's views, which dominated the study of U.S. history until the 1930s and remained influential to the midtwentieth century. More recently, scholars have sought to rescue the study of America's past from the mythology of the West and the historiography of the frontier.

The attention accorded to Turner's frontier thesis overshadowed his other contributions to scholarship and his evolutionary, multicausal perspective of history. In an 1891 essay titled "The Significance of History" (1891), he encouraged American historians to study all aspects of the past, including cultural, social, and economic influences, and to use the tools of the modern social sciences—including statistics—to explain political behavior. He also believed that there is no definitive historical work or single correct point of view, but that history is an "ongoing encounter between past and present," rewritten by each generation in response to contemporary issues. In his 1925 essay "The Significance of the Section in American History," Turner stressed the importance of studying specific sections, or regions, in American history and of examining the variety of political, economic, and cultural forces behind their formation. He expanded that view in *The Significance of Sections in American History* (1932), a book for which he was awarded the Pulitzer Prize for History posthumously in 1933.

Frederick Jackson Turner died on March 14, 1932, in Pasadena, California, where he had moved for health reasons. At the time of his death, he was working on a study of sectionalism at the Henry E. Huntington Library in nearby San Marino. Aside from his thesis on the American frontier, Turner is known for modernizing the study of history by focusing on the social forces that underlie political behavior and through the use of interdisciplinary methods.

Christina Rabe Seger

◇◇

"The Significance of the Frontier in American History" (excerpt), 1893

◇◇

In a landmark paper delivered at the World's Columbian Exposition in Chicago—which commemorated the four-hundredth anniversary of Christopher Columbus's arrival in the New World—historian Frederick Jackson Turner presented a novel theory on the evolution of core American beliefs and institutions. The origin, success, and very identity of the United States, he asserted, were direct results of the frontier experience of hundreds of thousands of migrating people and the hardships they endured over decades of westward expansion. "To the frontier," Turner wrote, "the American intellect owes its striking characteristics." His theory lent resonance to the Census Bureau's announcement in 1890 of the "closing of the frontier" and guided the teaching of American history for decades.

In a recent bulletin of the Superintendent of the Census for 1890 appear these significant words: "Up to and including 1880 the country had a frontier of settlement, but at present the unsettled area has been so broken into by isolated bodies of settlement that there can hardly be said to be a frontier line. In the discussion of its extent, its westward movement, etc., it can not, therefore, any longer have a place in the census reports." This brief official statement marks the closing of a great historic movement. Up to our own day American history has been in a large degree the history of the colonization of the Great West. The existence of an area of free land, its continuous recession, and the advance of American settlement westward, explain American development.

Behind institutions, behind constitutional forms and modifications, lie the vital forces that call these organs into life and shape them to meet changing conditions. The peculiarity of American institutions is, the fact that they have been compelled to adapt themselves to the changes of an expanding people—to the changes involved in crossing a continent, in winning a wilderness, and in developing at each area of this progress out of the primitive economic and political conditions of the frontier into the complexity of city life. Said Calhoun in 1817, "We are great, and rapidly—I was about to say fearfully—growing!" So saying, he touched the distinguishing feature of American life. All peoples show development; the germ theory of politics has been sufficiently emphasized. In the case of most nations, however, the development has occurred in a limited area; and if the nation has expanded, it has met other growing peoples whom it has conquered. But in the case of the United States we have a different phenomenon. Limiting our attention to the Atlantic coast, we have the familiar phenomenon of the evolution of institutions in a limited area, such as the rise of representative government; into complex organs; the progress from primitive industrial society, without division of labor, up to manufacturing civilization. But we have in addition to this a recurrence of the process of evolution in each western area reached in the process of expansion. Thus American development has exhibited not merely advance along a single line, but a return to primitive conditions on a continually advancing frontier line, and a new development for that area. American social development has been continually beginning over again on the frontier. This perennial rebirth, this fluidity of American life, this expansion westward with its new opportunities, its continuous touch with the simplicity of primitive society, furnish the forces dominating American character. The true point of view in the history of this nation is not the Atlantic coast, it is the Great West. Even the slavery struggle, which is made so exclusive an object of attention by writers like Professor von Holst, occupies its important place in American history because of its relation to westward expansion.

In this advance, the frontier is the outer edge of the wave—the meeting point between savagery and civilization. Much has been written about the frontier from the point of view of border warfare and the chase, but as a field for the serious study of the economist and the historian it has been neglected.

The American frontier is sharply distinguished from the European frontier—a fortified boundary line running through dense populations. The most significant thing about the American frontier is, that it lies at the hither edge of free land. In the census reports it is treated as the margin of that settlement which has a density of two or more to the square mile. The term is an elastic one, and for our purposes does not need sharp definition. We shall consider the whole frontier belt including the Indian country and the outer margin of the "settled area" of the census reports. This paper will make no attempt to treat the subject exhaustively; its aim is simply to call attention to the frontier as a fertile field for investigation, and to suggest some of the problems which arise in connection with it.

In the settlement of America we have to observe how European life entered the continent, and how America modified and developed that life and reacted on Europe. Our early history is the study of European germs developing in an American environment. Too exclusive attention has been paid by institutional students to the Germanic origins, too little to the American factors. The frontier is the line of most rapid and effective Americanization. The wilderness masters the colonist. It finds him a European in dress, industries, tools, modes of travel, and thought. It takes him from the

The advance of the frontier has meant a steady movement away from the influence of Europe, a steady growth of independence on American lines.

railroad car and puts him in the birch canoe. It strips off the garments of civilization and arrays him in the hunting shirt and the moccasin. It puts him in the log cabin of the Cherokee and Iroquois and runs an Indian palisade around him. Before long he has gone to planting Indian corn and plowing with a sharp stick, he shouts the war cry and takes the scalp in orthodox Indian fashion. In short, at the frontier the environment is at first too strong for the man. He must accept the conditions which it furnishes, or perish, and so he fits himself into the Indian clearings and follows the Indian trails. Little by little he transforms the wilderness, but the outcome is not the old Europe, not simply the development of Germanic germs, any more than the first phenomenon was a case of reversion to the Germanic mark. The fact is, that here is a new product that is American. At first, the frontier was the Atlantic coast. It was the frontier of Europe in a very real sense. Moving westward, the frontier became more and more American. As successive terminal moraines result from successive glaciations, so each frontier leaves its traces behind it, and when it becomes a settled area the region still partakes of the frontier characteristics. Thus the advance of the frontier has meant a steady movement away from the influence of Europe, a steady growth of independence on American lines. And to study this advance, the men who grew up under these conditions, and the political, economic, and social results of it, is to study the really American part of our history. . . .

First, we note that the frontier promoted the formation of a composite nationality for the American people. The coast was preponderantly English, but the later tides of continental immigration flowed across to the free lands. This was the case from the early colonial days. The Scotch-Irish and the Palatine Germans, or "Pennsylvania Dutch," furnished the dominant element in the stock of the colonial frontier. With these peoples were also the freed indented servants, or redemptioners, who at the expiration of their time of service passed to the frontier. Governor Spotswood of Virginia writes in 1717, "The inhabitants of our frontiers are composed generally of such as have been transported hither as servants, and, being out of their time, settle themselves where land is to be taken up and that will produce the necessarys of life with little labour." Very generally these redemptioners were of non-English stock. In the crucible of the frontier the immigrants were Americanized, liberated, and fused into a mixed race, English in neither nationality nor characteristics. The process has gone on from the early days to our own. Burke and other writers in the middle of the eighteenth century believed that Pennsylvania was "threatened with the danger of being wholly foreign in language, manners, and perhaps even inclinations." The German and Scotch-Irish elements in the frontier of the South were only less great. In the middle of the present century the German element in Wisconsin was already so considerable that leading publicists looked to the creation of a German state out of the commonwealth by concentrating their colonization. Such examples teach us to beware of misinterpreting the fact that there is a common English speech in America into a belief that the stock is also English.

In another way the advance of the frontier decreased our dependence on England. The coast, particularly of the South, lacked diversified industries, and was dependent on England for the bulk of its supplies. In the South there was even a dependence on the Northern colonies for articles of food. Governor Glenn, of South Carolina, writes in the middle of the eighteenth century: "Our trade with New York and Philadelphia was of this sort, draining us of all the little money and bills we could gather from other places for their bread, flour, beer, hams, bacon, and other things of their produce, all which, except beer, our new townships begin to supply us with, which are settled with very industrious and thriving Germans. This no doubt diminishes the number of shipping and the appearance of our trade, but it is far from being a detriment to us. Before long the frontier created a demand for merchants. As it retreated from the coast it became less and less possible for England to bring her supplies directly to the consumer's wharfs, and carry away staple crops, and staple crops began to give way to diversified agriculture for a time. The effect of this phase of the frontier action upon the northern section is perceived when we realize how the advance of the frontier aroused seaboard cities like Boston, New York, and Baltimore, to engage in rivalry for what Washington called 'the extensive and valuable trade of a rising empire.' The growth of nationalism and the evolution of American political institutions were dependent on the advance of the frontier. . . ."

It was [the] nationalizing tendency of the West that transformed the democracy of Jefferson into the national republicanism of Monroe and the democracy of Andrew Jackson. The West of the War of 1812, the West of Clay, and Benton and Harrison, and Andrew Jackson, shut off by the Middle States and the mountains from the coast sections, had a solidarity of its own with national tendencies. On the tide of the Father of Waters, North and South met and mingled into a nation. Interstate migration went steadily on—a process of cross-fertilization of ideas and institutions. The fierce struggle of the sections over slavery on the western frontier does not diminish the truth of this statement;

it proves the truth of it. Slavery was a sectional trait that would not down, but in the West it could not remain sectional. It was the greatest of frontiersmen who declared: "I believe this Government can not endure permanently half slave and half free. It will become all of one thing or all of the other." Nothing works for nationalism like intercourse within the nation. Mobility of population is death to localism, and the western frontier worked irresistibly in unsettling population. The effect reached back from the frontier and affected profoundly the Atlantic coast and even the Old World.

But the most important effect of the frontier has been in the promotion of democracy here and in Europe. As has been indicated, the frontier is productive of individualism. Complex society is precipitated by the wilderness into a kind of primitive organization based on the family. The tendency is anti-social. It produces antipathy to control, and particularly to any direct control. The tax-gatherer is viewed as a representative of oppression. Prof. Osgood, in an able article, has pointed out that the frontier conditions prevalent in the colonies are important factors in the explanation of the American Revolution, where individual liberty was sometimes confused with absence of all effective government. The same conditions aid in explaining the difficulty of instituting a strong government in the period of the confederacy. The frontier individualism has from the beginning promoted democracy. . . .

From the conditions of frontier life came intellectual traits of profound importance. The works of travelers along each frontier from colonial days onward describe certain common traits, and these traits have, while softening down, still persisted as survivals in the place of their origin, even when a higher social organization succeeded. The result is that to the frontier the American intellect owes its striking characteristics. That coarseness and strength combined with acuteness and inquisitiveness; that practical, inventive turn of mind, quick to find expedients; that masterful grasp of material things, lacking in the artistic but powerful to effect great ends; that restless, nervous energy; that dominant individualism, working for good and for evil, and withal that buoyancy and exuberance which comes with freedom—these are traits of the frontier, or traits called out elsewhere because of the existence of the frontier. Since the days when the fleet of Columbus sailed into the waters of the New World, America has been another name for opportunity, and the people of the United States have taken their tone from the incessant expansion which has not only been open but has even been forced upon them. He would be a rash prophet who should assert that the expansive character of American life has now entirely ceased. Movement has been its dominant fact, and, unless this training has no effect upon a people, the American energy will continually demand a wider field for its exercise. But never again will such gifts of free land offer themselves. For a moment, at the frontier, the bonds of custom are broken and unrestraint is triumphant. There is not *tabula rasa.* The stubborn American environment is there with its imperious summons to accept its conditions; the inherited ways of doing things are also there; and yet, in spite of environment, and in spite of custom, each frontier did indeed furnish a new field of opportunity, a gate of escape from the bondage of the past; and freshness, and confidence, and scorn of older society, impatience of its restraints and its ideas, and indifference to its lessons, have accompanied the frontier. What the Mediterranean Sea was to the Greeks, breaking the bond of custom, offering new experiences, calling out new institutions and activities, that, and more, the ever retreating frontier has been to the United States directly, and to the nations of Europe more remotely. And now, four centuries from the discovery of America, at the end of a hundred years of life under the Constitution, the frontier has gone, and with its going has closed the first period of American history.

Sources: American Studies at the University of Virginia (http://xroads.virginia.edu); Frederick Jackson Turner, *The Frontier in American History* (New York: Henry Holt and Company, 1921).

Twain, Mark
(1835–1910)

Samuel Langhorne Clemens, writing under the pen name Mark Twain after 1863, was a self-taught humorist, novelist, travel writer, lecturer, and polemicist who became an American cultural icon and international celebrity. Over the course of a career that would span more than 40 years, he brought to American letters an ear for the vernacular, a down-to-earth perspective, and a sometimes jaundiced eye on social mores that transformed the nation's literature and popular consciousness. A son of the frontier and satirist of the Gilded Age, he explored some of the most colorful locations and most sensitive issues of his time with an irreverent humor, egalitarian spirit, and insight into character that earned several of his works a place in the literary canon.

Early Life and Influences

The first major American writer to emerge from the Western frontier rather than the Eastern Seaboard, Clemens was born on November 30, 1835, in Florida, Missouri. The family moved to nearby Hannibal, a small town fronting the Mississippi River, when he was 4. His formal education ended upon the death of his father in 1847, when Clemens quit school and joined his brother Orion's printing business as an apprentice. By age 14, he was working on Orion's newspaper, the *Hannibal Journal,* as a printer and editorial assistant.

While his adolescent life was made difficult by the family's precarious economic circumstances, Clemens's experiences on the Mississippi would provide the source for some of his most beloved works: *The Adventures of Tom Sawyer* (1876) and *Adventures of Huckleberry Finn* (1884)—episodic novels brought to life by their free-flowing idiomatic language, undercurrents of social satire, and characters who would attain near-mythic status in American culture—and *Life on the Mississippi* (1883), an account of his later days as a steamboat pilot.

Clemens left home in 1853 and spent the next four years working as a printer in St. Louis, New York City, Philadelphia, and Cincinnati. In 1857, he landed in New Orleans, where he apprenticed in the art of steamboat piloting, obtained his license, and practiced the occupation until the Civil War closed the Mississippi River to traffic in 1861.

Western Years and Rise to Prominence

With the riverboats and his life at a standstill, Clemens set out by stagecoach for Carson City, Nevada, with his brother Orion, who had been appointed territorial secretary. As the Civil War raged back East, Clemens tried his hand at gold and silver prospecting, failing at both, and took up writing for the *Territorial Express* in the mining town of Virginia City, Nevada. He signed his early columns, a mix of straight reporting and humor, with the byline "Josh"; in February 1863, he adopted the pseudonym Mark Twain, old riverboat slang for the sounding depth of two fathoms.

After moving to San Francisco, where he continued his work as a journalist and partnered with humorist and editor Bret Harte, Twain had his breakthrough as a writer with publication of his humorous tall tale "The Celebrated Jumping Frog of Calaveras County," in the New York *Saturday Press* on November 18, 1865. The story gained national attention and launched Twain on his multifaceted career. He followed "The Celebrated Jumping Frog" with sketches for a number of magazines and newspapers, including Harte's *Californian,* and in 1866 traveled to Hawaii as a correspondent for the *Sacramento Union.* With material gathered on the trip, he made his debut as a lecturer upon returning to California.

As Twain's writing expanded from reporting, humor, and local-color sketches to travelogues, personal reminiscences, and fiction, the many sides of his temperament began to shine through. Ever sensitive, human, and irresistibly charming, his writing at times also shocked readers with its irreverence toward authority, social convention, and organized religion as well as his caustic attacks on any number of injustices, abominations, peeves, and execrations. His first best-selling book, *The Innocents Abroad* (1869), epitomized that irreverence with his chronicle of an 1867 voyage to Europe and the Holy Land in which he skewers Old World grandiosity. A prequel, *Roughing It* (1872), is an equally humorous if less biting travel narrative based on his experiences in the Wild West during the 1860s. Twain took aim at English history and culture in two satirical works cast as novels for younger readers, *The Prince and the Pauper* (1882) and *A Connecticut Yankee in King Arthur's Court* (1889). Privilege, pretense, greed, and hypocrisy were objects of his vitriol wherever he found them.

Fame, Fortune, *The Gilded Age*, and Late Sorrows

Twain's rise from obscurity to celebrity was accompanied almost simultaneously by his elevation from rags to riches. The latter was accelerated by his marriage in 1870 to Olivia "Livy" Langdon, the wealthy daughter of a coal magnate from Elmira, New York. The couple lived in Buffalo until the following year, when they moved to Hartford, Connecticut, and began building the lavishly appointed Victorian mansion in which they would spend the next 17 years. (Harriet Beecher Stowe lived next door.) Twain and Livy Clemens remained married for 34 years, until her death in 1904. They had four children, a son born in 1872 who died a year and a half later and three daughters born in Hartford. Twain later called his years in Hartford the happiest and most productive of his life. It was there that he wrote most of his best-known books.

The Gilded Age: A Tale of Today (1873), a novel co-authored with friend and neighbor Charles Dudley Warner, is not usually ranked among Twain's finest works, but its title provided an apt characterization—and enduring label—for the period of frenetic materialism, public corruption, and social pretension in the United States during the last quarter of the nineteenth century. In colorful and amusing episodes, *The Gilded Age* evokes the schemes and excesses, feverish speculation, and carnivalesque atmosphere of the post–Civil War era in which Clemens lived and wrote. Set in Washington, D.C., the novel is part romantic melodrama and part social satire, with multiple plots and subplots, a throng of characters, and several themes. The heart of the novel, however, is the authors' satirical thrusts at venality in the halls of power, unscrupulous lobbying practices, corporate malfeasance, the

A humorist of depth, irony, conscience, and sheer comic genius, Mark Twain has been called the first writer to achieve a uniquely American voice. Late in life, however, the course of public affairs and personal tragedy cast him into a dark and pessimistic state.

affectations of the newly rich, and the middle-class obsession with material success.

Clemens himself was both dismayed by and attracted to the pursuit of wealth. While he assailed the country's materialism in print, he sometimes viewed himself more as a businessman than as a writer. And while he indicted plutocrats mercilessly, he lived in luxury (at least until encountering financial difficulties) and hobnobbed socially with captains of industry. Captivated by the latest technology, he invested in such innovations as a steam generator, an engraving process called Kaolotype, a carpet-weaving machine, and several of his own patents. He lost money in a publishing venture called Charles L. Webster and Company—which issued *Huckleberry Finn* and General Ulysses S. Grant's *Personal Memoirs* (1885–1886)—and finally lost everything in a failed typesetting invention called the Paige Compositor.

Bankrupt in 1891, Twain closed the Hartford house and moved with his family to Europe. There he embarked upon a prodigious round of writing and publication to restore his wealth. In 1895, the family joined him on a yearlong, round-the-world lecture tour that ultimately paid off his debts and provided the material for his last travel book, *Following the Equator* (1897). Back in America, he lectured extensively and published stories and essays primarily.

Twain's disposition and late writings took a decidedly dark turn, beginning with a period of depression following the death of his eldest daughter, Susy, of meningitis in 1896. Livy died of a heart attack in June 1904 after a long illness, and his youngest daughter, Jean, succumbed to a seizure in December 1909. The losses left Twain in a state of permanent despondency and pessimism, as reflected in the essay "What Is Man?" (1906). Late writings also conveyed an ardent anti-imperialism and pacifism.

Twain died of a heart attack on April 21, 1910, at his home in Redding, Connecticut. His last work was a lengthy, rambling autobiography, largely dictated to a stenographer; the first of a projected three volumes was published in 2010 to mark the hundredth anniversary of his death.

Donald D. Kummings and Sueann M. Wells

See also: Huckleberry Finn; Realism

◇◇

"The War Prayer," 1905

◇◇

One of Mark Twain's last works, "The War Prayer" is a scathing condemnation of armed conflict, especially in the name of patriotism or religion. Written in outrage and disgust after the Spanish-American War (1898) and Philippine-American War (1899–1902), the prose poem was rejected for publication upon completion in 1905 because of its radical viewpoint. "I don't think the prayer will be published in my time," Twain wrote to a friend. "None but the dead are permitted to tell the truth." He was right. The piece was not published until 1923, long after Twain's death and the end of World War I. In those war-weary, isolationist times, "The War Prayer" was more in tune with public sentiment. It became a classic of pacifist literature.

It was a time of great and exalting excitement. The country was up in arms, the war was on, in every breast burned the holy fire of patriotism; the drums were beating, the bands playing, the toy pistols popping, the bunched firecrackers hissing and spluttering; on every hand and far down the receding and fading spread of roofs and balconies a fluttering wilderness of flags flashed in the sun; daily the young volunteers marched down the wide avenue gay and fine in their new uniforms, the proud fathers and mothers and sisters and sweethearts cheering them with voices choked with happy emotion as they swung by; nightly the packed mass meetings listened, panting, to patriot oratory which stirred the deepest deeps of their hearts, and which they interrupted at briefest intervals with cyclones of applause, the tears running down their cheeks the while; in the churches the pastors preached devotion to flag and country, and invoked the God of Battles beseeching His aid in our good cause in outpourings of fervid eloquence which moved every listener. It was indeed a glad and gracious time, and the half dozen rash spirits that ventured to disapprove of the war and cast a doubt upon its righteousness straightway got such a stern and angry warning that for their personal safety's sake they quickly shrank out of sight and offended no more in that way.

Sunday morning came—next day the battalions would leave for the front; the church was filled; the volunteers were there, their young faces alight with martial dreams—visions of the stern advance, the gathering momentum, the rushing charge, the flashing sabers, the flight of the foe, the tumult, the enveloping smoke, the fierce pursuit, the surrender! Then home from the war, bronzed heroes, welcomed, adored, submerged in golden seas of glory! With the volunteers sat their dear ones, proud, happy, and envied by the neighbors and friends who had no sons and brothers to send forth to the field of honor, there to win for the flag, or, failing, die the noblest of noble deaths. The service proceeded; a war chapter from the Old Testament was read; the first prayer was said; it was followed by an organ burst that shook the building, and with one impulse the house rose, with glowing eyes and beating hearts, and poured out that tremendous invocation

God the all-terrible!
Thou who ordainest!
Thunder thy clarion
and lightning thy sword!

Then came the "long" prayer. None could remember the like of it for passionate pleading and moving and beautiful language. The burden of its supplication was, that an ever-merciful and benignant Father of us all would watch over our noble young soldiers, and aid, comfort, and encourage them in their patriotic work; bless them, shield them in the day of battle and the hour of peril, bear them in His mighty hand, make them strong and confident, invincible in the bloody onset; help them to crush the foe, grant to them and to their flag and country imperishable honor and glory—

An aged stranger entered and moved with slow and noiseless step up the main aisle, his eyes fixed upon the minister, his long body clothed in a robe that reached to his feet, his head bare, his white hair descending in a frothy cataract to his shoulders, his seamy face unnaturally pale, pale even to ghastliness. With all eyes following him and wondering, he made his silent way; without pausing, he ascended to the preacher's side and stood there waiting. With shut lids the preacher, unconscious of his presence, continued with his moving prayer, and at last finished it with the words, uttered in fervent appeal, "Bless our arms, grant us the victory, O Lord our God, Father and Protector of our land and flag!"

The stranger touched his arm, motioned him to step aside— which the startled minister did—and took his place. During some moments he surveyed the spellbound audience with solemn eyes, in which burned an uncanny light; then in a deep voice he said:

"I come from the Throne—bearing a message from Almighty God!" The words smote the house with a shock; if the stranger perceived it he gave no attention. "He has heard the prayer of His servant your shepherd, and will grant it if such shall be your desire after I, His messenger, shall have explained to you its import—that is to say, its full import. For it is like unto many of the prayers of men, in that it asks for more than he who utters it is aware of—except he pause and think.

"God's servant and yours has prayed his prayer. Has he paused and taken thought? Is it one prayer? No, it is two—one uttered, the other not. Both have reached the ear of Him Who heareth all supplications, the spoken and the unspoken. Ponder this— keep it in mind. If you would beseech a blessing upon yourself, beware! lest without intent you invoke a curse upon a neighbor at the same time. If you pray for the blessing of rain upon your crop which needs it, by that act you are possibly praying for a curse upon some neighbor's crop which may not need rain and can be injured by it.

"You have heard your servant's prayer—the uttered part of it. I am commissioned of God to put into words the other part of it—that part which the pastor—and also you in your hearts— fervently prayed silently. And ignorantly and unthinkingly? God grant that it was so! You heard these words: 'Grant us the victory, O Lord our God!' That is sufficient. *The whole* of the uttered prayer is compact into those pregnant words. Elaborations were not necessary. When you have prayed for victory you have prayed for many unmentioned results which follow victory—*must* follow it, cannot help but follow it. Upon the listening spirit of God fell also the unspoken part of the prayer. He commandeth me to put it into words. Listen!

"O Lord our Father, our young patriots, idols of our hearts, go forth to battle—be Thou near them! With them—in spirit—we also go forth from the sweet peace of our beloved firesides to smite the foe. O Lord our God, help us to tear their soldiers to bloody shreds with our shells; help us to cover their smiling fields with the pale forms of their patriot dead; help us to drown the thunder of the guns with the shrieks of their wounded, writhing in pain; help us to lay waste their humble homes with a hurricane of fire; help us to wring the hearts of their unoffending widows with unavailing grief; help us to turn them out roofless with little children to wander unfriended the wastes of their desolated land in rags and hunger and thirst, sports of the sun flames of summer and the icy winds of winter, broken in spirit, worn with travail, imploring Thee for the refuge of the grave and denied it—for our sakes who adore Thee, Lord, blast their hopes, blight their lives, protract their bitter pilgrimage, make heavy their steps, water their way with their tears, stain the white snow with the blood of their wounded feet! We ask it, in the spirit of love, of Him Who is the Source of Love, and Who is the ever-faithful refuge and friend of all that are sore beset and seek His aid with humble and contrite hearts. Amen.

(*After a pause.*) "Ye have prayed it; if ye still desire it, speak! The messenger of the Most High waits!"

It was believed afterward that the man was a lunatic, because there was no sense in what he said.

Source: Harper's Monthly, November 1916.

Wharton, Edith
(1862–1937)

The preeminent fictional chronicler of Old New York society, novelist and short-story writer Edith Wharton produced elegant, ironic descriptions of changing class conventions, relations between the sexes, and the institution of marriage during the belle epoque of the late nineteenth century. Written at a time when the old moneyed aristocracy was being displaced by *nouveau riche* industrialists and financiers, such acclaimed Wharton novels as *The House of Mirth* (1905) and *The Age of Innocence* (1920) balanced satire and psychological insight in probing the frail humanity and moral hypocrisy underlying upper-class custom, courtesy, and tradition. Wharton's work is often compared to that of Henry James, a longtime friend and mentor, for its mannered fluency and finely honed depictions of an orderly world.

Born Edith Newbold Jones on January 24, 1862, she was descended from two prominent and wealthy New York families. (It has been suggested that the expression "keeping up with the Joneses" was coined in reference to her father's family.) She was privately educated, spent five years with her family traveling in Europe, and, according to biographers, had a somewhat lonely childhood in which she made up stories to entertain herself. She began writing poems and short stories as a teenager and completed her first novella before making her society debut at age 17.

In 1885, she married Edward "Teddy" Wharton of Boston, a banker and older man who began suffering bouts of depression; the marriage lasted 28 years, many of them unhappy and apart. In the meantime, Wharton took up writing as a profession with the encouragement of several friends, including Henry James. Throughout her life, in marriage and thereafter, she managed to

The novels of Edith Wharton provide an ironic, finely honed insider's view of social convention, human frailty, and moral hypocrisy in American high society during the mid-1800s—just as it was being displaced by new-money industrialists and financiers.

combine her four great passions in life: literature, travel, society, and interior design.

Wharton published the first of her many short stories, titled "Mrs. Manstey's View," in *Scribner's Magazine* in 1891. Over the course of the next four decades, a steady flow of her stories would appear in such other respected publications as *The Atlantic Monthly, Century Magazine,* and *Harper's.* By the time she achieved her first popular success with *The House of Mirth* in 1905, she had already published six short-story collections, three novels, and two volumes on Victorian-style design and Italian gardens and villas.

A number of biographers and literary critics have noted correspondences between Wharton's literature and her personal experiences. Her portrayal of matrimony as a kind of incarceration—a central theme of her two most acclaimed works, the short novel *Ethan Frome* (1911) and *The Age of Innocence*—no doubt drew on her own unhappy marriage. She also knew something of the scandal of divorce, after leaving Teddy Wharton in 1913, and understood the psychology of extramarital love from two relationships of her own. Above all, perhaps, she was a perceptive observer of her society peers and their milieu.

The highly popular *Ethan Frome,* an anomalous work for Wharton in tone and setting, is a brutal tragedy of frustrated passion set in a fictional New England town reminiscent of Lenox in western Massachusetts, where Wharton spent many summers. *The Age of Innocence,* a subtle unveiling of the emotional world of her youth, is about the plight of a high-society New York couple trapped by tradition, old money, and prior romantic obligations. The novel won the 1921 Pulitzer Prize for Fiction, making Wharton the first woman to be so honored.

Until 1907, Wharton divided her time between New York City and the estate she built and decorated in Lenox, called The Mount (now a National Historic Landmark). She took up year-round residence at The Mount after the dissolution of her marriage and then moved permanently to France. She did extensive volunteer relief work in Paris during World War I, for which she was awarded the Cross of the Legion of Honor by the French government. She later moved to a villa in the nearby town of Saint-Brice-sous-Forêt and spent winters in Hyères on the French Riviera. Among the last of Wharton's nearly 50 books was an autobiography titled *A Backward Glance* (1934). She died of a stroke at Saint-Brice on August 11, 1937.

Beth Kreydatus and Jeff Hacker

See also: James, Henry

◇◇

Chapter One, *The Age of Innocence,* 1920

◇◇

Edith Wharton's Pulitzer Prize–winning novel of manners The Age of Innocence *portrays the lifestyle, values, and rigid conventions of New York's upper crust in the 1870s with a keen but ironic eye. Chapter One evokes the time, place, and social milieu with an ideal setting—the opera—and introduces several of the main characters: Newland Archer, a prospering young lawyer; May Welland, his new fiancée; her grandmother, Mrs. Manson Mingott; and other members of her family. Upon reading the first part of the manuscript, Wharton's editor wrote to her: "Congratulations upon this opening section of 'The Age of Innocence.' You have caught the flavor of Old New York in the days when it possessed some social cohesion, and have pictured a bygone period when it was not a series of disconnected villages."*

On a January evening of the early seventies, Christine Nilsson was singing in Faust at the Academy of Music in New York.

Though there was already talk of the erection, in remote metropolitan distances "above the Forties," of a new Opera House which should compete in costliness and splendour with those of the great European capitals, the world of fashion was still content to reassemble every winter in the shabby red and gold boxes of the sociable old Academy. Conservatives cherished it for being small and inconvenient, and thus keeping out the "new people" whom New York was beginning to dread and yet be drawn to; and the sentimental clung to it for its historic associations, and the musical for its excellent acoustics, always so problematic a quality in halls built for the hearing of music.

It was Madame Nilsson's first appearance that winter, and what the daily press had already learned to describe as "an exceptionally brilliant audience" had gathered to hear her, transported through the slippery, snowy streets in private broughams, in the spacious family landau, or in the humbler but more convenient "Brown *coupé.*" To come to the Opera in a Brown *coupé* was almost as honourable a way of arriving as in one's own carriage; and departure by the same means had the immense advantage of enabling one (with a playful allusion to democratic principles) to scramble into the first Brown conveyance in the line, instead of waiting till the cold-and-gin congested nose of one's own coachman gleamed under the portico of the Academy. It was one of the great livery-stableman's most masterly intuitions to have discovered that Americans want to get away from amusement even more quickly than they want to get to it.

When Newland Archer opened the door at the back of the club box the curtain had just gone up on the garden scene. There was no reason why the young man should not have come earlier, for he had dined at seven, alone with his mother and sister, and had lingered afterward over a cigar in the Gothic library with glazed black-walnut bookcases and finial-topped chairs which was the only room in the house where Mrs. Archer allowed smoking. But, in the first place, New York was a metropolis, and perfectly aware that in metropolises it was "not the thing" to arrive early at the opera; and what was or was not "the thing" played a part as important in Newland Archer's New York as the inscrutable totem terrors that had ruled the destinies of his forefathers thousands of years ago.

The second reason for his delay was a personal one. He had dawdled over his cigar because he was at heart a dilettante, and thinking over a pleasure to come often gave him a subtler satisfaction than its realisation. This was especially the case when the pleasure was a delicate one, as his pleasures mostly were; and on this occasion the moment he looked forward to was so rare and exquisite in quality that—well, if he had timed his arrival in accord with the prima donna's stage-manager he could not have entered the Academy at a more significant moment than just as she was singing: "He loves me—he loves me not—*he loves me!*—" and sprinkling the falling daisy petals with notes as clear as dew.

She sang, of course, "*M'ama!*" and not "he loves me," since an unalterable and unquestioned law of the musical world required that the German text of French operas sung by Swedish artists should be translated into Italian for the clearer understanding of English-speaking audiences. This seemed as natural to Newland Archer as all the other conventions on which his life was moulded: such as the duty of using two silver-backed brushes with his monogram in blue enamel to part his hair, and of never appearing in society without a flower (preferably a gardenia) in his buttonhole.

"*M'ama . . . non m'ama . . .*" the prima donna sang, and "*M'ama!,*" with a final burst of love triumphant, as she pressed the dishevelled daisy to her lips and lifted her large eyes to the sophisticated countenance of the little brown Faust-Capoul, who was vainly trying, in a tight purple velvet doublet and plumed cap, to look as pure and true as his artless victim.

Newland Archer, leaning against the wall at the back of the club box, turned his eyes from the stage and scanned the opposite side of the house. Directly facing him was the box of old Mrs. Manson Mingott, whose monstrous obesity had long since made it impossible for her to attend the Opera, but who was always represented on fashionable nights by some of the younger members of the family. On this occasion, the front of the box was filled by her daughter-in-law, Mrs. Lovell Mingott, and her daughter, Mrs. Welland; and slightly withdrawn behind these brocaded matrons sat a young girl in white with eyes ecstatically fixed on the stage lovers. As Madame Nilsson's "*M'ama!*" thrilled out above the silent house (the boxes always stopped talking during the Daisy Song) a warm pink mounted to the girl's cheek, mantled her brow to the roots of her fair braids, and suffused the young slope of her breast to the line where it met a modest tulle tucker fastened with a single gardenia. She dropped her eyes to the immense bouquet of lilies-of-the-valley on her knee, and Newland Archer saw her white-gloved finger-tips touch the flowers softly. He drew a breath of satisfied vanity and his eyes returned to the stage.

No expense had been spared on the setting, which was acknowledged to be very beautiful even by people who shared his acquaintance with the Opera houses of Paris and Vienna.

What was or was not "the thing" played a part as important in Newland Archer's New York as the inscrutable totem terrors that had ruled the destinies of his forefathers thousands of years ago.

The foreground, to the footlights, was covered with emerald green cloth. In the middle distance symmetrical mounds of woolly green moss bounded by croquet hoops formed the base of shrubs shaped like orange-trees but studded with large pink and red roses. Gigantic pansies, considerably larger than the roses, and closely resembling the floral pen-wipers made by female parishioners for fashionable clergymen, sprang from the moss beneath the rose-trees; and here and there a daisy grafted on a rose-branch flowered with a luxuriance prophetic of Mr. Luther Burbank's far-off prodigies.

In the centre of this enchanted garden Madame Nilsson, in white cashmere slashed with pale blue satin, a reticule dangling from a blue girdle, and large yellow braids carefully disposed on each side of her muslin chemisette, listened with downcast eyes to M. Capoul's impassioned wooing, and affected a guileless incomprehension of his designs whenever, by word or glance, he persuasively indicated the ground floor window of the neat brick villa projecting obliquely from the right wing.

"The darling!" thought Newland Archer, his glance flitting back to the young girl with the lilies-of-the-valley. "She doesn't even guess what it's all about." And he contemplated her absorbed young face with a thrill of possessorship in which pride in his own masculine initiation was mingled with a tender reverence for her abysmal purity. "We'll read Faust together . . . by the Italian lakes . . ." he thought, somewhat hazily confusing the scene of his projected honey-moon with the masterpieces of literature which it would be his manly privilege to reveal to his bride. It was only that afternoon that May Welland had let him guess that she "cared" (New York's consecrated phrase of maiden avowal), and already his imagination, leaping ahead of the engagement ring, the betrothal kiss and the march from Lohengrin, pictured her at his side in some scene of old European witchery.

He did not in the least wish the future Mrs. Newland Archer to be a simpleton. He meant her (thanks to his enlightening companionship) to develop a social tact and readiness of wit enabling her to hold her own with the most popular married women of the "younger set," in which it was the recognised custom to attract masculine homage while playfully discouraging it. If he had probed to the bottom of his vanity (as he sometimes nearly did) he would have found there the wish that his wife should be as worldly-wise and as eager to please as the married lady whose charms had held his fancy through two mildly agitated years; without, of course, any hint of the frailty which had so nearly marred that unhappy being's life, and had disarranged his own plans for a whole winter.

How this miracle of fire and ice was to be created, and to sustain itself in a harsh world, he had never taken the time to think out; but he was content to hold his view without analysing it, since he knew it was that of all the carefully-brushed, white-waistcoated, button-hole-flowered gentlemen who succeeded each other in the club box, exchanged friendly greetings with him, and turned their opera-glasses critically on the circle of ladies who were the product of the system. In matters intellectual and artistic Newland Archer felt himself distinctly the superior of these chosen specimens of old New York gentility; he had probably read more, thought more, and even seen a good deal more of the world, than any other man of the number. Singly they betrayed their inferiority; but grouped together they represented "New York," and the habit of masculine solidarity made him accept their doctrine on all the issues called moral. He instinctively felt that in this respect it would be troublesome—and also rather bad form—to strike out for himself.

"Well—upon my soul!" exclaimed Lawrence Lefferts, turning his opera-glass abruptly away from the stage. Lawrence Lefferts was, on the whole, the foremost authority on "form" in New York. He had probably devoted more time than any one else to the study of this intricate and fascinating question; but study alone could not account for his complete and easy competence. One had only to look at him, from the slant of his bald forehead and the curve of his beautiful fair moustache to the long patent-leather feet at the other end of his lean and elegant person, to feel that the knowledge of "form" must be congenital in any one who knew how to wear such good clothes so carelessly and carry such height with so much lounging grace. As a young admirer had once said of him: "If anybody can tell a fellow just when to wear a black tie with evening clothes and when not to, it's Larry Lefferts." And on the question of pumps versus patent-leather "Oxfords" his authority had never been disputed.

"My God!" he said; and silently handed his glass to old Sillerton Jackson.

Newland Archer, following Lefferts's glance, saw with surprise that his exclamation had been occasioned by the entry of a new figure into old Mrs. Mingott's box. It was that of a slim young woman, a little less tall than May Welland, with brown hair growing in close curls about her temples and held in place by a narrow band of diamonds. The suggestion of this head-dress, which gave her what was then called a "Josephine look," was carried out in the cut of the dark blue velvet gown rather theatrically caught up under her bosom by a girdle with a large old-fashioned clasp. The wearer of this unusual dress, who seemed quite unconscious of the attention it was attracting, stood a moment in the centre of the box, discussing with Mrs. Welland the propriety of taking the latter's place in the front right-hand corner; then she yielded with a slight smile, and seated herself in line with Mrs. Welland's sister-in-law, Mrs. Lovell Mingott, who was installed in the opposite corner.

Mr. Sillerton Jackson had returned the opera-glass to Lawrence Lefferts. The whole of the club turned instinctively, waiting to hear what the old man had to say; for old Mr. Jackson was as great an authority on "family" as Lawrence Lefferts was on "form." He knew all the ramifications of New York's cousin-ships; and could not only elucidate such complicated questions as that of the connection between the Mingotts (through the Thorleys) with the Dallases of South Carolina, and that of the relationship of the elder branch of Philadelphia Thorleys to the Albany Chiverses (on no account to be confused with the Manson Chiverses of University Place), but could also enumerate the leading characteristics of each family: as, for instance, the fabulous stinginess of the younger lines of Leffertses (the Long Island ones); or the fatal tendency of the Rushworths to make foolish matches; or the insanity recurring in every second generation of the Albany Chiverses, with whom their New York cousins had always refused to intermarry—with the disastrous exception of poor Medora Manson, who, as everybody knew . . . but then her mother was a Rushworth.

In addition to this forest of family trees, Mr. Sillerton Jackson carried between his narrow hollow temples, and under his soft thatch of silver hair, a register of most of the scandals and mysteries that had smouldered under the unruffled surface of New York society within the last fifty years. So far indeed did his information extend, and so acutely retentive was his memory, that he was supposed to be the only man who could have told you who Julius Beaufort, the banker, really was, and what had become of handsome Bob Spicer, old Mrs. Manson Mingott's father, who had disappeared so mysteriously (with a large sum of trust money) less than a year after his marriage, on the very day that a beautiful Spanish dancer who had been delighting thronged audiences in the old Opera-house on the Battery had taken ship for Cuba. But these mysteries, and many others, were closely locked in Mr. Jackson's breast; for not only did his keen sense of honour forbid his repeating anything privately imparted, but he was fully aware that his reputation for discretion increased his opportunities of finding out what he wanted to know.

The club box, therefore, waited in visible suspense while Mr. Sillerton Jackson handed back Lawrence Lefferts's opera-glass. For a moment he silently scrutinised the attentive group out of his filmy blue eyes overhung by old veined lids; then he gave his moustache a thoughtful twist, and said simply: "I didn't think the Mingotts would have tried it on."

Source: Edith Wharton, *The Age of Innocence* (New York: D. Appleton and Company, 1920).

Bibliography

Arthur, Anthony. *Radical Innocent: Upton Sinclair.* New York: Random House, 2006.

Auerbach, Jonathan. *Male Call: Becoming Jack London.* Durham, NC: Duke University Press, 1996.

Barnard, Ellsworth. *Edwin Arlington Robinson: A Critical Study.* New York: Octagon, 1969.

Barrish, Phillip J. *The Cambridge Introduction to American Literary Realism.* New York: Cambridge University Press, 2011.

Bass, Amy. *Those About Him Remained Silent: The Battle over W.E.B. Du Bois.* Minneapolis: University of Minnesota Press, 2009.

Benfey, Christopher E.G. *The Double Life of Stephen Crane.* New York: Alfred A. Knopf, 1992.

Benstock, Shari. *No Gifts from Chance: A Biography of Edith Wharton.* New York: Charles Scribner's Sons, 1994.

Berkove, Lawrence I. *A Prescription for Adversity: The Moral Art of Ambrose Bierce.* Columbus: Ohio State University Press, 2002.

Berryman, John. *Stephen Crane: A Critical Biography.* New York: Farrar, Straus and Giroux, 1977.

Best, Felton O. *Crossing the Color Line: A Biography of Paul Laurence Dunbar, 1872–1906.* Dubuque, IA: Kendall/Hunt, 1996.

Billington, Ray Allen. *Frederick Jackson Turner: Historian, Scholar, Teacher.* New York: Oxford University Press, 1973.

Bloom, Harold. *Stephen Crane.* New York: Chelsea House, 2002.

Bogue, Allan G. *Frederick Jackson Turner: Strange Roads Going Down.* Norman: University of Oklahoma Press, 1998.

Brady, Kathleen. *Ida Tarbell: Portrait of a Muckraker.* New York: Seaview/Putnam, 1984.

Buenker, John D., and Joseph Buenker, eds. *Encyclopedia of the Gilded Age and Progressive Era.* Armonk, NY: M.E. Sharpe, 2005.

Cady, Edwin H. *William Dean Howells: Dean of American Letters.* 2 vols. Syracuse, NY: Syracuse University Press, 1958.

Chalfant, Edward. *Better in Darkness: A Biography of Henry Adams: His Second Life, 1862–1891*. Hamden, CT: Archon, 1994.

Civello, Paul. *American Naturalism and Its Twentieth-Century Transformations*. Athens: University of Georgia Press, 1994.

Conder, John J. *Naturalism in American Fiction: The Classic Phase*. Lexington: University Press of Kentucky, 1984.

Davis, Linda H. *Badge of Courage: The Life of Stephen Crane*. Boston: Houghton Mifflin, 1998.

Donaldson, Scott. *Edwin Arlington Robinson: A Poet's Life*. New York: Columbia University Press, 2007.

Drabelle, Dennis. *The Great American Railroad War: How Ambrose Bierce and Frank Norris Took on the Notorious Central Pacific Railroad*. New York: St. Martin's, 2012.

Edel, Leon. *Henry James: A Life*. New York: Harper and Row, 1985.

Filler, Louis. *The Muckrakers*. University Park: Pennsylvania State University Press, 1976.

Fishkin, Shelley Fisher, ed. *A Historical Guide to Mark Twain*. New York: Oxford University Press, 2002.

Foner, Philip S., ed. *W.E.B. Du Bois Speaks*. 2 vols. New York: Pathfinder, 1970.

Freedman, Jonathan, ed. *The Cambridge Companion to Henry James*. New York: Cambridge University Press, 1998.

Goodman, Susan, and Carl Dawson. *William Dean Howells: A Writer's Life*. Berkeley: University of California Press, 2005.

Harris, Thomas E. *Analysis of the Clash over the Issues Between Booker T. Washington and W.E.B. Du Bois*. New York: Garland, 1993.

Howe, Irving. *Sherwood Anderson*. New York: Sloane, 1951.

Jewell, Andrew, and Janis Stout. *The Selected Letters of Willa Cather*. New York: Alfred A. Knopf, 2013.

Kaplan, Justin. *Mr. Clemens and Mark Twain, A Biography*. New York: Simon & Schuster, 1966.

Kershaw, Alex. *Jack London: A Life*. New York: St. Martin's, 1997.

Koupal, Nancy Tystad, ed. *Baum's Road to Oz: The Dakota Years*. Pierre: South Dakota State Historical Society, 2000.

Labor, Earle, and Jeanne Campbell Reesman. *Jack London*. New York: Twayne, 1994.

Langbaum, Robert Woodrow. *The Modern Spirit: Essays on the Continuity of Nineteenth and Twentieth Century Literature*. New York: Oxford University Press, 1970.

Lee, Hermione. *Edith Wharton*. New York: Alfred A. Knopf, 2007.

Lewis, David Levering. *W.E.B. Du Bois: Biography of a Race, 1868–1919*. New York: Henry Holt, 1993.

———. *W.E.B. Du Bois: The Fight for Equality and the American Century, 1919–1963.* New York: Henry Holt, 2000.

Lewis, R.W.B. *Edith Wharton: A Biography.* New York: Harper and Row, 1975.

Lindemann, Marilee, ed. *The Cambridge Companion to Willa Cather.* New York: Cambridge University Press, 2005.

Lingeman, Richard R. *Theodore Dreiser: An American Journey, 1908–1945.* New York: Putnam, 1990.

———. *Theodore Dreiser: At the Gates of the City, 1871–1907.* New York: Putnam, 1986.

Loving, Jerome. *The Last Titan: The Life of Theodore Dreiser.* Berkeley: University of California Press, 2005.

———. *Mark Twain: The Adventures of Samuel L. Clemens.* Berkeley: University of California Press, 2010.

Lubove, Roy. *The Progressives and the Slums: Tenement House Reform in New York City, 1890–1917.* Westport, CT: Greenwood, 1962.

Lundquist, James. *Jack London: Adventures, Ideas, and Fiction.* New York: Ungar, 1987.

Martin, Jay. *Harvests of Change: American Literature, 1865–1914.* Englewood Cliffs, NJ: Prentice-Hall, 1967.

Martin, Jay, and Gossie H. Hudson, eds. *The Paul Laurence Dunbar Reader.* New York: Dodd, Mead, 1975.

Matthiessen, F.O. *Henry James: The Major Phase.* New York: Oxford University Press, 1970.

———. *Theodore Dreiser.* New York: William Sloane, 1951.

Mattson, Kevin. *Upton Sinclair and the Other American Century.* Hoboken, NJ: John Wiley & Sons, 2006.

Mookerjee, R.N. *Art for Social Justice: The Major Novels of Upton Sinclair.* Metuchen, NJ: Scarecrow, 1988.

Morris, Roy, Jr. *Ambrose Bierce: Alone in Bad Company.* New York: Crown, 1995.

Novick, Sheldon M. *Henry James: The Mature Master.* New York: Random House, 2007.

———. *Henry James: The Young Master.* New York: Random House, 1996.

Owens, David M. *The Devil's Topographer: Ambrose Bierce and the American War Story.* Knoxville: University of Tennessee Press, 2006.

Pizer, Donald, ed. *The Cambridge Companion to American Realism and Naturalism: Howells to London.* New York: Cambridge University Press, 1995.

Powers, Ron. *Mark Twain: A Life.* New York: Free Press, 2005.

Quirk, Tom, and Gary Scharnhorst, eds. *American Realism and the Canon.* Wilmington: University of Delaware Press, 1994.

Railton, Ben. *Contesting the Past, Reconstructing the Nation: American Literature and Culture in the Gilded Age, 1876–1893.* Tuscaloosa: University of Alabama Press, 2007.

Rampersad, Arnold. *The Art and Imagination of W.E.B. Du Bois.* New York: Schocken, 1976.

Rideout, Walter B. *Sherwood Anderson: A Writer in America.* Madison: University of Wisconsin Press, 2006.

Rogers, Katherine. *L. Frank Baum, Creator of Oz: A Biography.* New York: St. Martin's, 2002.

Samuels, Ernest. *Henry Adams.* Cambridge, MA: Belknap, 1989.

Schwartz, Evan I. *Finding Oz: How L. Frank Baum Discovered the Great American Story.* New York: Houghton Mifflin Harcourt, 2009.

Shi, David E. *Facing Facts: Realism in American Thought and Culture, 1850–1920.* New York: Oxford University Press, 1995.

Shucard, Alan, Fred Moramarco, and William Sullivan. *Modern American Poetry, 1865–1950.* Boston: Twayne, 1989.

Singley, Carol. *Edith Wharton: Matters of Mind and Spirit.* New York: Cambridge University Press, 1995.

Smith, Harriet Elinor. *Autobiography of Mark Twain.* Berkeley: University of California Press, 2010.

Storey, Mark. *Rural Fictions, Urban Realities: A Geography of Gilded Age American Literature.* New York: Oxford University Press, 2013.

Sundquist, Eric J., ed. *American Realism: New Essays.* Baltimore: Johns Hopkins University Press, 1982.

Townsend, Kim. *Sherwood Anderson: A Biography.* Boston: Houghton Mifflin, 1987.

Trachtenberg, Alan. *The Incorporation of America: Culture and Society in the Gilded Age.* New York: Hill and Wang, 1982.

Valentine, Rebecca, ed. *Gilded Age and Progressive Era Reference Library: Primary Sources.* Detroit: UXL, 2007.

Van Doren, Mark. *Edwin Arlington Robinson*, New York: Haskell House, 1975.

Walcutt, Charles Child. *American Literary Naturalism: A Divided Stream.* Westport, CT: Greenwood, 1973.

Wills, Garry. *Henry Adams and the Making of America.* Boston: Houghton Mifflin, 2005.

Wilson, Harold S. *McClure's Magazine and the Muckrakers.* Princeton, NJ: Princeton University Press, 1970.

Woodress, James. *Willa Cather: A Literary Life.* Lincoln: University of Nebraska Press, 1987.

Ziff, Larzer. *The American 1890s: Life and Times of a Lost Generation.* New York: Viking, 1966.

Web Sites

DreiserWebSource, University of Pennsylvania Library: www.library.upenn.edu/collections/rbm/dreiser

Edith Wharton Society: http://public.wsu.edu/~campbelld/wharton/index.html

Henry James Society: http://mockingbird.creighton.edu/english/HJS/home.html

Horatio Alger Digital Serials Project, Northern Illinois University Libraries: www.ulib.niu.edu

Jack London Online Collection: http://london.sonoma.edu

Kate Chopin International Society: www.katechopin.org

Literature.org, The Online Literature Library: www.literature.org

Literature Network: www.online-literature.com

Mark Twain Project Online: www.marktwainproject.org

Paul Laurence Dunbar Web Site, University of Dayton: www.dunbarsite.org

Poetry Foundation: www.poetryfoundation.org

Sharpe Online Reference: www.sharpe-online.com

W.E.B. Du Bois Online Resources, Library of Congress: www.loc.gov/rr/program/bib/dubois

Willa Cather Foundation: www.willacather.org

William Dean Howells Society: http://public.wsu.edu/~campbelld/howells

Index

Page numbers followed by "*i*" indicate illustrations.

Alamance Community College
Library
P.O. Box 8000
Graham, NC 27253